HOW TO UNDERSTAND AND USE

DISPLAY

by Haruhisa Hattori

装幀＝大貫伸樹＋伊藤庸一＋経田　林

Book Design＝Shinju Onuki＋Yoichi Ito＋Rin Tsuneda

HOW TO UNDERSTAND AND USE DISPLAY
Copyright © 1988 Graphic-sha Publishing Co., Ltd.
1-9-12 Kudankita, Chiyoda-ku, Tokyo 102, Japan.

Printed in Japan

First Printing, May 1988

目 次

第1章 ディスプレイ ——————— 2
第2章 空間 ——————— 4
第3章 情報 ——————— 6
第4章 演出 ——————— 9
第5章 演出の材料 ——————— 18
　　　人間 ——————— 18
　　　人の動作 ——————— 26
　　　人の気配 ——————— 32
　　　人形 ——————— 34
　　　仮面 ——————— 38
　　　光 ——————— 42
　　　色 ——————— 50
　　　かたち ——————— 56
　　　動き ——————— 64
　　　緊張感 ——————— 72
　　　たくさん ——————— 78
　　　ファンタジー ——————— 82
　　　スポーツ ——————— 88
　　　季節の風物 ——————— 94
　　　季節の行事 ——————— 100
　　　不思議 ——————— 112
　　　エキゾチシズム ——————— 116
　　　ノスタルジア ——————— 120
第6章 管理 ——————— 128
第7章 評価 ——————— 130

CONTENTS

1) DISPLAY ——————— 12
2) SPACE ——————— 13
3) INFORMATION ——————— 14
4) PRODUCTION ——————— 16
5) MATERIALS FOR PRODUCTION - 18
　　HUMANS ——————— 18
　　MOVEMENT OF PEOPLE ——————— 26
　　APPEARENCE OF PEOPLE ——————— 32
　　DOLLS ——————— 34
　　MASKS ——————— 38
　　LIGHTING ——————— 42
　　COLORS ——————— 50
　　SHAPES ——————— 56
　　MOVEMENT ——————— 64
　　A FELLING OF TENTION ——————— 72
　　PLENTIFULLNESS ——————— 78
　　FANTASY ——————— 82
　　SPORTS ——————— 88
　　SEASONAL FEATURES ——————— 94
　　SEASONAL EVENTS ——————— 100
　　MYSTERY ——————— 112
　　EXOTICISM ——————— 116
　　NOSTALGIA ——————— 120
6) MANAGEMENT ——————— 131
7) VALUATION ——————— 132

ディスプレイとは

ディスプレイ（display）という言葉はショーウインドウ・ディスプレイとかエキジビション・ディスプレイといったように商いの場でおなじみのものです。また，美術館や博物館でもよく使われる言葉です。しかし，それだけではありません。祭りのディスプレイとか地位のディスプレイといったように生活の場や仕事の場でも使われていますし，さらに，計器類の表示やコンピューターの画像表示，動物の求愛表現や威嚇表現もディスプレイと呼んでいます。このように，いろいろな場で使われているディスプレイという言葉，一体どんな意味をもっているのでしょうか。

言葉の意味を知るには，その語源を調べてみる必要があるでしょう。ダヴィッド社刊の「ディスプレイ小辞典」（森 崇，寺澤勉共著）によるとディスプレイの語源はラテン語の displicāre になるといわれています。この言葉は「たたんであるものを開く」という行いを表わしています。するとこの行いを考えてみれば，ディスプレイというものがわかるはずです。

そこで，まず考えられることは空間の存在です。つまり，ディスプレイには空間がつきものということです。

次に，この行いは，内側を見せることと考えられます。内側を見せることは，特別に見せることでしょう。そこから「示す」とか「誇示する」という意味が生まれてきたのです。

この「示す」とか「誇示する」という行いは，知らせたいという強い欲求が生み出すものでしょう。そして，その欲求は情報があるから生まれてくるのです。つまり，ディスプレイには情報もつきものなのです。

さらに，この行いは，見る側の反応を求める表現と考えることができます。そして，その表現を生み出すことが演出です。つまり，ディスプレイには演出もつきものなのです。

このように，ディスプレイという言葉の語源を探ることから「空間」「情報」「演出」の三つの言葉が生まれてきました。

展示とは

ディスプレイという言葉にあたる日本語として「展示」という言葉が使われています。この言葉を探ってみることも，ディスプレイを知るためには必要でしょう。この「展示」の「展」という文字は「ひろげる」という行いを表わしています。「示」という文字は「机の上に置く」という行いを表わしています。この二つを重ねると「ひろげたり，机の上にのせたりする」という行いになります。この行いのためには空間が必要でしょう。また，この行いには，見せたいという強い欲求を感じることができます。そして，この行いは見る人の反応を求める表現行為でもあります。とすると，この展示という言葉からも先のディスプレイと同じように「空間」「情報」「演出」の三つの言葉が浮かび上ってくるのです。

そこで，この本では，この三つの言葉を追い求めることによって，ディスプレイというものを明らかにしていくことにしました。

ディスプレイの目的と特性

情報を伝えることは，その情報の受け手の反応を求めることでしょう。

反応とは，働きかけに対して起こる動きのことです。とすると，ディスプレイが求めるものは，情報の受け手の動きということになります。

この動きは，ディスプレイの場や種類によって異なります。商いの場のディスプレイが求めるものは情報の受け手の購買行動でしょう。美術館や博物館のディスプレイが求めるのは観賞行動と学習行動です。祭りのディスプレイは気分の解放と集団の結束を求め，地位のディスプレイが求めるのは従属でしょう。計器類や画像の表示は適格な操作を求め，動物の求愛ディスプレイは愛情行為を，威嚇ディスプレイは縄張りからの退去を求めるものです。このように，それぞれのディスプレイは，それぞれに行動を求めるのです。その点を，まずはっきりとさせておく必要があります。

ディスプレイは多くの特性をもっています。その特性の多くは，空間をメディアにしていることから生まれているといっていいでしょう。ここに，その特性のうち，ディスプレイだけがもっているものをあげてみましょう。

五感に訴える

人間の五感とは，視覚，聴覚，嗅覚，触覚，味覚の五つの感覚のことです。そして，人間は空間に包まれて生活をしています。その空間をメディアにするということは，これらのすべての感覚に訴えることができるということです。何故なら，視覚と触覚と味覚の三つの感覚が対象とするものは，空間に存在するからです。また，聴覚が対象とする音，嗅覚が対象とする臭いは空間によって伝えられるものだからです。

参加が得られる

ディスプレイには場があります。この場があるということは，人の参加が得られるということです。そして，参加するということは，積極的に情報を受けようとすることです。人がこのような状態にあるとき，情報は容易に伝わります。

また，この参加者は，情報を受けて反応し，時には質問を投げかけます。その態度や言葉から，参加者の欲求をつかみとることができます。つまり，情報のフィード・バックがあるのです。

さらに，この参加するということは，体験することです。体験することは，最も印象が強いことといっていいでしょう。

ものに近い

ディスプレイの場には，商品や資料や作品といったものが目の前にあります。時には，そのものを手でさわることもできます。これは情報の本体に近いということでしょう。このような状況にあるとき，情報は容易に伝わります。何故なら，近いということは，コミュニケーションを効果的にする最も大きな要素だからです。身近な事件が，遠くの大事件よりも強い印象をもつことは，よく経験することです。

人間が介在する

ディスプレイの場には，人間が介在する場合が多いものです。例えば，商いの場には販売員が，美術館や博物館には説明員が居ます。これらの人間が，情報を強調したり，補ったりします。このように近くで，しかも人間の口から直に伝えられる情報には暖かさを感じることができますし，信頼感も生まれやすいものです。

場が固定されている

ディスプレイの場は固定されていることが多いものです。このことは，決してメディアとしての弱さには結びつきません。よく「ここだけの話だけどね」という話しかけが，多くの人に向かって話しかけるよりも強い伝達力をもつことがあります。つまり，固定されていることは，使い方によって力になるということです。

最後の場のメディア

情報を伝える活動には，いろいろなものがあります。例えば商いの場でも広告，ダイレクトメール，パブリシティなどがあります。購買行動を考えてみた場合，ディスプレイは，これらの中では最後に働きかけるものといっていいでしょう。これは，ディスプレイが，先の活動を利用することができるということです。利用するとは，情報を反復することによって印象を強めることです。

また，ディスプレイは，先に行われる情報活動を本体に結びつける働きももっています。とすると，ディスプレイによってフォローされない情報活動は，本体への結びつきが弱いということになるわけです。

このように，ディスプレイには，このメディアだけがもつ多くの特性があります。これらの特性のひとつひとつをよく知り，それを活用することが，ディスプレイの力を発揮させるための重要なカギになるのです。

第2章　空間

商いの場

私達は空間に対して，よく「場」という言葉を使います。生活空間のことを生活の場，商業空間のことを商いの場といったように。この場という言葉には，空間そのものを指す「場所」の意味と，空間の使われ方を指す「場合」の意味の二つがあります。ディスプレイは，この場所と場合の両方に関係しています。すると，ここでは，空間という言葉ではなく場という言葉を使った方がよいようです。

さて，身のまわりには，いろいろな場があります。先にあげた生活の場，商いの場，さらに仕事の場，教育の場，公共の場，祭りの場といったように。そして，それぞれの場でディスプレイが行われています。

しかし，これらの場の中で，ディスプレイが大きな役割を果たしているのは商いの場でしょう。そこで，ここでは，とくに商いの場をとりあげ，そのディスプレイの方法を説明していきましょう。

商いの場は，飲食を商う場，サービスを商う場，ものを商う場の三つに分けることができます。これらの中で，とくにディスプレイが強く要求されるのはものを商う場でしょう。そこで，その場についての話が多くなります。

ものを商う場とは店のことでしょう。店には大きく分けて二つの働きがあります。その一つは店を「見世」とも書くことからもわかるように見せる働きです。この働きは，ものを生産者から消費者へ移転させるという商業目的に深く関係しているものです。

次に，店を「タナ」と呼ぶことがあります。これは棚に通じ，ものを貯える働きを表わしています。この働きはものの生産と消費とのズレを調節するという商業目的に結びついているのです。

この二つの働きのうち，ディスプレイを必要とするものは，もちろん見せる働きですが，この見せるためのディスプレイにも二つに分けて考えることができます。

その一つは，商品をピック・アップし，それを際立てて見せる方法，或いは何らかの仕掛けによって空間に意味を加える方法です。この方法にはトークン・ディスプレイ（token）という言葉があります。

もう一つは，商品を分類し，その分類毎にあつめて，わかりやすく，また比較しやすいように見せる方法です。この方法にはアソートメント・ディスプレイ（assortment）という言葉があります。

ところが，一般に商いの場でディスプレイといった場合，先にあげたトークン・ディスプレイを指す場合が多いようです。

このトークン・ディスプレイの場がショー・スペースです。この場は二つに分けて考えられます。一つは店の外部に対して働きかけるショーウインドウ。もう一つは店の内部にあって働きかけをするショースペースです。この二つの場について，さらに詳しく説明しましょう。

ショーウインドウ

ショーウインドウは，よく「店の顔」と呼ばれます。この呼名が，この場の重要性を物語っています。顔は人にとって重要なものでしょう。ショーウインドウは店にとって，この顔のように重要なもの，ということです。たしかに，ショーウインドウは店を訪れる人が最初に目にする場であり，最も目立つ場であり，最も多くの人が目にする場でもあるのです。重要なものであるのは当然でしょう。

では，この重要な場は，一体どんな働きをするのでしょうか。

情報を伝える働き

ディスプレイの基本的な働きである情報伝達を，まずはじめにあげることができます。この場を通じて，商品について，店について，時期について，催しものについて，生活についてなど，いろいろな情報を伝えるのです。店では最も目立つ場だけに，その効果には大きなものがあるでしょう。

誘引と選別の働き

街を行く人の目を捉え，興味をもたせ，店の中に誘引する働きと，店の性格を表現することによって，店に入る人を選別する働きです。この二つの働きは，店の性格によって使い分けることになります。できるだけ多くの人に入ってもらいたい誘引型の店と，扱い商品に欲望をもった人だけに入ってもらいたい選別型の店との使い分けです。

商品を販売する働き

この場は，商品がとくに際立ってみえる場です。また，閉店した後でも商品を目にすることができる場です。そこで，当然，商品は売れるわけです。ウインドウ・ショッピングという言葉が，この働きをよく表わしています。

ショースペース

人をもてなす働き

　この場は，もてなしを表わす場でもあるのです。もてなしとは，人に対して好意と敬意を表わすことでしょう。そして人の関心に応えることでもあるのです。この場は表現の容易な場です。また，変化をさせやすい場です。それだけに，趣向をこらして，もてなしを表現するためには，恰好の場といえるでしょう。

話題づくりの働き

　趣向をこらした表現は，人の関心をあつめます。そして話題になります。その話題は，いろいろなメディアを通じて大きく広がっていくでしょう。それは店名を広く伝えることにつながります。店は話題になっていなければなりません。その話題をつくり出す上で，この場は大きな力を発揮するのです。

街の景観をつくる働き

　この場は，街に向かって開かれています。そして，街はショーウインドウの連なりとみることができるでしょう。すると，この場のディスプレイは街の景観をつくることになります。店は街に依存しています。依存しているからには，街に貢献する義務があります。この場によって街の景観をつくることは，この義務を果たすための恰好の材料なのです。

　ショーウインドウには，このように多くの働きがあります。これらのうち，どの働きに力を入れるかは，店の性格，場所，ショーウインドウのサイズ，かたち，そして，時期によって違ってきます。ディスプレイの作業にあたっては，それらをよく見極めることが重要です。この条件に合わないディスプレイの効果は期待できないでしょう。

　売場の中にあって，働きかけをする場ですが，店によって，いろいろな呼び方があります。VP（Visual Presentation）スペース，PP（Point of Presentation）スペース，見世場，マグネット，集視ポイントなど。

　また，そのかたちにもいろいろなものがあります。フロアーの上で，壁面で，天井から吊して，といったように。

　その設備もまた，ステージ，テーブル，棚，パネル，ガラスケース，ワゴンなど，いろいろとあります。

　では，このスペースは，一体どんな働きをするのでしょうか。

商品のありかを知らせる働き

　売場での客の質問の大部分は商品のありかについてです。販売員が，その煩雑な作業から逃れるためには，商品のありかを示すものが必要です。そこで，この場を使い，代表する商品を目立つように掲げ，そのありかを，はっきりと示すのです。

売場の性格を知らせる働き

　売場に特別の性格をもたせることがあります。その性格は，客に知らせなければ意味がありません。その知らせる働きをするのがこの場の役割です。ディスプレイによって，性格をわかりやすく表現し，知らせるのです。そして，欲求を引き出すのです。

商品を説明する働き

　売場には，特別に知らせたい商品があります。例えば新しく入荷した商品，流行の商品，戦略的な商品などです。その商品を，この場で説明するのです。その機能，性能，使い方，組み合わせ方，或いは，その材料，産地，製造方法，そして雰囲気などです。このディスプレイは，生活のトレンドを知らせることにもつながります。

催しものを知らせる働き

　売場には，販売を促進するための催しものがいろいろとあります。その催しものを知らせることも，この場の役割です。さらに，その催しものの雰囲気を盛り上げることも，この場のディスプレイの大切な働きなのです。

売場に鮮度を出す働き

　この場は変化させやすいことが特徴です。そこで，この場のディスプレイを多彩に変化させ，新鮮な印象を保つのです。その印象は，周囲の売場の印象にもつながります。

売場ににぎわい感を出す働き

　この場のディスプレイを華やいだものにすれば，その周囲に，にぎわい感が生まれます。このにぎわい感は，人の気分を高めるばかりでなく，人をあつめる役割を果たします。そのあつまった人は，さらに売場に，にぎわい感を加えるのです。

客をもてなす働き

　売場は，客を迎える場です。それだけに，もてなしを表現するものが，無ければなりません。その働きをするのがこの場です。ショーウインドウと同じように，趣向をこらしたディスプレイによって，見る人の気分を高めるのです。

客を動かす働き

　この場を，売場の中に点在させることによって，客を誘導します。この誘導の目的は，商品との接触機会を多くすることですが，それだけではありません。人は動いている時に積極性が生まれ，行動的になります。購買行動を促すことがディスプレイの目的ですから，この働きも見逃すわけにはいきません。

第3章　情報

情報とは

　情報時代とか情報化社会とかいわれています。それだけに情報に対する関心は，大変に高いものがあるようです。

　では，情報とは，一体どんなものなのでしょうか。

　情報というものを，文字から探ってみますと，「情」という文字には「こころ」の意味があります。「報」には「知らせ」の意味があります。この二つを重ねてみますと，情報とは「こころが動かされる知らせ」ということになります。

　では，人がこころを動かされるのは，一体どんな時でしょうか。それは，多分，知らせに対して効用を感じた時でしょう。

　そして，効用を感じるとは，欲求に合っていると感じることです。

　とすると，単なる知らせは情報ではないことになります。それは，情報のための材料ということになるでしょう。

情報の材料

　情報をつくるためには，まず，その材料をあつめなければなりません。商いの場には，情報のためのいろいろな材料があります。商品に関する材料，時期に関する材料，店に関する材料，催しものに関する材料，生活に関する材料などです。それぞれについて，ここに考えられるものをあげてみましょう。

商品に関する情報の材料

　商品には，いろいろな効用があります。それらが情報のための材料といっていいでしょう。この効用は使用的効用と記号的効用の二つに分けて考えることができます。

1）使用的効用

　これは使用目的，使いやすさ，安全性，快適さといったものに関係した効用です。用途，機能，性能，材料，質感，色彩，サイズ，形態，製造方法，使用する時間，使用する場所，使用する機会，使用対象などがあげられます。

2）記号的効用

　その多くは象徴性とか誇示とかいったことに関係した効用です。ブランド，メーカー，作家，産地，雰囲気，様式，由来などがあげられます。

　店が商品をつくったり，商品を揃えたりするときには，必ず意図をもちます。その意図とは，これらの効用の中のどの部分に重点を置くかということでしょう。商品に関する情報をつくるためには，その点を見極めることから始めなければなりません。

時期に関する情報の材料

商品を時期に合わせて揃えるのが店の役目です。また、生活を送る上で、時期というものは大きな役割を果たしています。そこから、時期というものも情報になるのです。ここに、店と生活に関わりのある時期についてあげてみましょう。

1）行事の時期

季節の行事、社会の行事、地域の行事、国家の行事、家族の行事など。

2）祝いの時期

全快、出産、入学、卒業、成人、長寿、新築、受勲など。

3）見舞の時期

暑中、寒中、火事、入院など。

4）贈り物の時期

年賀、中元、歳暮、クリスマスなど。

5）入荷の時期

商品の新入荷、旬のものの入荷、流行商品の入荷など。

6）買得の時期

時期というものには、由来のある場合が多いようです。その由来の中にも関心を呼ぶものが数多くあるでしょう。それらも、また情報のための優れた材料です。

店に関する情報の材料

商品を選ぶ前に、店選びをするのが一般的なショッピングのかたちです。そこで、店についての情報が必要になってきます。そのための材料としては、次のようなものがあげられます。

1）店の立地、環境に関するもの

場所、建物、インテリアなど

2）店の性格に関するもの

営業日、営業時間、扱い商品の種類、扱い商品の価格帯、代表商品、対象とする客層、店の歴史など。

3）店のサービスに関するもの

パッケージのサービス、配送や代行のサービス、景品のサービスなど。

今、店は、はっきりとした主張をもたなければならないといわれています。独自の主張のある生活を求める人びとが、店にもそれを求めているからでしょう。店に関する情報は、この主張に通じるのです。

催しものに関する情報の材料

店は、いろいろな催しものを開きます。この催しものは、あくまでも販売を促進することが目的ですが、そのために情報を強めて伝え、人をあつめ、にぎわい感をつくるのです。その材料としては次のようなものがあげられます。

1）タイトルや目的など内容に関するもの。

2）開催の日時や期間など時期に関するもの。

3）場所や規模など場に関するもの。

生活に関する情報の材料

店は、生活に密接に結びついていなければなりません。そして、生活の水先案内の役割を果たさなければなりません。そこで、生活に関わる情報が必要になるのです。その情報の材料になるものは、政治から経済、歴史、海外の動きなどあらゆるものがあげられます。生活には、周囲にあるものすべてが影響を与えるからです。そこで広くアンテナを張っていなければなりません。そして、速やかに情報の材料をつかまえなければなりません。

情報づくり

　このように，商いの場には，沢山の材料があります。この中から情報をつくり出すためには，何らかの根拠に従って選別をしなければなりません。その根拠になるものの一つが人びとの欲求です。この欲求も，人によっていろいろなものがありますが，基本的なものとしては，次のようなものがあげられます。
- ●本能に根ざしたもの
- ●自己を表現するもの
- ●他人と差別をつけるもの
- ●快楽をもたらすもの
- ●こころと感性を豊かにするもの
- ●知識を豊かにするもの
- ●好奇心を満足させるもの
- ●所有欲を満足させるもの

　これらの欲求は，環境や時代によって差が生まれます。それを見極めることが必要です。

　次に，これらの欲求を掘り下げ，具体的なかたちでつかまえなければなりません。そのために役立つのがヒットしているものや流行，関心事などです。これらは人びとの欲求が，具体的に表われたものとみていいからです。

　また，雑誌やテレビや映画のシーンも参考になります。これらは，人びとが頭の中に描いているシーンを具体化したものといっていいからです。人は，欲求を頭の中にシーンとして描くといわれているのですから。

　購買動機というものも情報選びの根拠の一つです。質がいいから，流行のものだから，長もちするから，或いは，ギフトのために，といったようにいろいろな動機が考えられます。

　店が対象としている客層について，その特徴を調べてみることも必要でしょう。層によって欲求に違いがあるからです。

　さらに，競合する店，周囲の店，時期なども情報選びの根拠になるでしょう。

　これらの根拠に従って，先にあげた材料の中から，情報を選び出します。その情報を，さらに組み合わせたり，何かを加えたりして効用のあるものに仕立てあげます。

　存在感というものがあります。「存在感のある人」とか「存在感のあるもの」といった具合に使いますが，これは無視できない人やモノについて語る言葉です。

　無視できないとは，こころが動かされることでしょう。すると，この存在感も情報の一つと考えることができそうです。そこで，存在感のある店，存在感のある建物，存在感のあるディスプレイというものが求められるのです。

情報がつくり出すもの

　店は多くの情報を送り出します。人は，それらを受けとめ，それらが積み重なり，店に対して思い込みをつくります。それがイメージです。このイメージは人の行動を左右する大きな力をもっています。それだけに大切に扱わなければなりません。

　情報の積み重ねがイメージをつくり出すならば，情報を操作することによって，イメージも操作することができそうです。そこで，店にとって望ましいイメージを考え，それに合わせて情報を管理する必要がでてきます。いま，盛んに行われているCI（Corporate Identity）は，このイメージの操作を目的とした活動です。

　ディスプレイもまた，その望ましいイメージを目標にして，すべてが考えられなければならないのです。

第4章　演出

　演出とは，見る人の反応を求め，さまざまなものを駆使して行う表現のことでしょう。商いの場のディスプレイは，このために，装置，商品，照明，小道具，音響を駆使します。時には，ここににおいが加わることもあるでしょう。人間が登場することもあります。

　では，何を表現するのでしょうか。

　一つは，気分を高めるものです。そして，もう一つは具体的な情報です。

　では，気分を高めるものとは，一体何でしょうか。

楽しさ

　まずはじめに，楽しさがあげられます。そして，その楽しさの一つに，目に対する刺激をあげることができます。例えば，光るもの，輝くもの，鮮やかな色，動き，盛り沢山，面白いかたち，といったものです。

　物語も楽しさをつくり出すものの一つです。とくに夢の世界を表現したファンタジーは，楽しさのあふれたものといっていいでしょう。

　見世物の世界も楽しさの宝庫です。とくにこの世界のスター達。道化師はその代表格，ディスプレイの場で活躍させたい材料の一つです。

　さらに，スポーツの世界，祭り，さらに，エキゾチシズムのあるもの，ノスタルジアのあるものなど，楽しさの素材は身のまわりにいっぱいあります。

　この楽しさを，さらに大きくするためには，意外性が必要です。意外性とは，思いがけないもの，思いがけない組み合わせ，思いがけないストーリー，といったものでしょう。トリックとかマジックの楽しさも，意外性がつくり出すのです。

　この楽しさは，情報を伝えるためにも欠かせません。情報は，楽しさというオブラートで包まれなければ，なかなか伝わらないからです。やはり，楽しさとは，ディスプレイの世界では，最も重要な働き手といっていいでしょう。

親しさ

　親しさを感じた時も気分が高まります。この親しさとは，共感がつくり出すものでしょう。そして，共感とは，欲求に対して応えがあったときに感ずるもののようです。たとえば，興味をもったものが用意されている，関心のある情報が流される，好きな感覚のものがあるといったように。

　そこで，共感づくりのために，ディスプレイのテーマに，関心の高いものをもってくるのです。行事やニュースや季節感がそれです。とくに，人間をテーマにしたものは，効果が高いようです。人が最も関心をもつのは人間だからです。

　流行の雰囲気や時代の感覚を表現するのも共感をつくり出すことが目的です。ファッションの要素や新しいアートのテクニックは，この時代感覚の表現には，恰好のものといっていいでしょう。

　この親しさもまた，情報を伝えるためには欠かせません。親しい人の言うことは，すぐに受け入れるでしょう。そこからも，親しさというものの効果がわかります。

美しさ

　美しさも，気分を高めるためには欠かせません。ところが，この美しさというもの，人の主観によるものだけに，とらえるのがなかなか難しいようです。しかし，古い昔から，黄金比というものが使われてきたことからもわかるように，多くの人に，共通して感じられる美しさがあるようです。

　これについては，昔から，いろいろな人がいろいろな説を唱えてきました。その中に共通してあらわれているものに「秩序」とか「統一」という言葉と，それに対する「複雑」とか「変化」という言葉があります。これらの言葉が表わしているものが美しさに関係するのでしょう。

　「秩序」「統一」という言葉が表わしているものには，揃える，整える，繰り返す，順序立てる，釣り合いをとる，といったものがあげられます。

　「複雑」「変化」という言葉が表わしているものには，動かす，対比する，強調する，といったものが考えられます。

　この二つの対立したものを組み合わせることによって美しさは生み出せるでしょう。

品性の高さ

　この美しさに，質の高さを結びつけたものが品性の高さでしょう。この品性の高さもまた，気分を高めるもののようです。

　では，質の高さとは何でしょうか。

　それは，多分，恵まれた環境と多くの人の知恵と手と美意識によって生まれてくるものでしょう。

　やはり，人の気分を高めるには，人の知恵，人の手，人の美意識，がふんだんに必要なようです。

もてなしの表現

　ここにあげた，気分を高めるための表現は，もてなしの表現といいかえることができそうです。何故なら，もてなしとは，好意と敬意をあらわすことでしょう。そして，関心のあるものを提供することです。それは，すべて，楽しさ，親しさ，美しさ，品の良さ，に結びつくからです。

　商いの場とは，客を迎える場です。そこには，もてなしは，絶対に欠かせないものです。そこで，もてなしの表現が重要になるのです。

情報を伝えるために

　ディスプレイでは，情報の表現を考えるとともに，情報を伝えやすくすることも考えなければなりません。そのために，いろいろな技術を使います。その主なものを，ここにあげてみましょう。

目を捉える

　情報を伝えるためには，まず目を捉えることが必要です。そのために，仕掛けを用意します。アイ・キャッチャーとかアテンション・ゲッターと呼ばれているものです。これは，目を刺激するものといっていいでしょう。刺激的な光と輝き，動くもの，動きを感じるもの，鮮やかな色彩，刺激的なかたち，不思議なもの，思いがけないもの，思いがけない組み合わせなど，いろいろとあります。

　これらは，楽しさをつくりだす要素でもありました。とすると，楽しさとは，アイ・キャッチャーでもあるわけです。

集中させる

　積極的に見てくれるように仕向けることです。そのためには，見やすさが必要でしょう。見やすい位置，見やすい照明，見やすい背景を考えてください。

　手に取りやすさを考えることもあります。触覚が意識の集中に役立つからです。

　周囲の視覚的な雑音を取り去ることも必要です。煩雑に見えるとき，人の意識は散漫になります。とくに，売場は，いろいろな商品といろいろな設備がつくりだす混沌とした場です。整理をして見せる必要があるでしょう。

鮮度を感じさせる

　情報は新しさが生命です。そこで，新しさを感じさせることが必要になるのです。目先を変えるのは，そのための最も手軽な方法です。位置，背景，色彩，器具，小道具，揃え方，組み合わせ方など，目先を変える要素はいろいろとあります。といっても，プログラムをつくって，計画的に変えることが必要です。無駄な変化は効果を小さくするからです。

　新しい商品を目立たせることも一つの方法でしょう。看板やショーカードを添えて新製品であることを強調してください。

　話題やニュースに合わせて見せることも考えていいでしょう。この場合は，対応の早さが重要，そこで，変化のしやすさが求められるのです。

明解にする

　ディスプレイは，その前を通り過ぎる一瞬の勝負です。そこから，分かりやすさが求められるのです。また，人は煩雑さを嫌います。とくに，近頃のように忙しい世の中になると，煩雑さは，ますます嫌われるようになります。

　分かりやすいディスプレイのためには，伝えたい情報をはっきりとつかむことが必要です。自分で分からなくて，どうして他人が分かってくれるでしょうか。

　情報を絞りこみ，焦点をはっきりとさせることも必要です。人は多くのことを，同時に受け入れることはできないからです。

　読ませることも重要です。文字は意味が，はっきりとしているからです。また，信頼感もあります。読みやすさ，わかりやすさを考えて，魅力的な文章を用意してください。

臨場感を出す

　臨場感とは，あたかもその場にいるような感じをもつこと。ディスプレイでは，情景をつくることによって，その感じは出せるでしょう。この方法は大きな力をもっています。商品は使われている状態にあるとき，本来の魅力を発揮するからです。また，使い方の説明にもなるからです。

　それだけではありません。人間は，欲求を頭の中に情景として描くといわれています。その情景を目の当たりにするわけですから，こんなに刺激的なことはありません。

　また，情景を目にすることは，体験したような錯覚を起こします。疑似体験とはいえ，体験することは欲望が刺激されることです。そして，強く印象にのこることです。

相乗効果を図る

　相乗効果とは二つ以上の力を合わせることによって，大きな効果を引き出すことです。ディスプレイは，この働きを発揮させやすいメディアの一つです。それは，購買行動のための最後の場で働きかけるというディスプレイの特性からくるのです。

　この効果を出すためには，ディスプレイ以外の情報活動の表現について知っておかなければなりません。そして，その活用を考えなければなりません。例えば広告，その表現と同じ表現や同じスローガン，同じキャラクター，同じシンボルをディスプレイに使うのです。この方法によって，ディスプレイの場で，広告を思い出させるのです。人は目にしたことの大部分は忘れてしまいます。ところが，何らかのきっかけがあると，かなりの部分を思い出します。そのきっかけをディスプレイがつくるのです。そして，これは情報を反復して伝えることになるのです。大きな効果につながることは間違いないでしょう。

1) DISPLAY

What is a display?

The word display is most often used in the business world to describe such things as show-windows or exhibitions. It is also used by the art world and museums. However, there are other places that it is also used; it can be used in our daily lives and at our workplaces to describe such things as festivals and rankings, and it is also utilized to sum up the visual aspect of calculators and computers. Furthermore, it is used to explain the degree of emotion that animals use during courtship and in times of danger. So what in fact does this word "display" mean in general?

It is necessary to study the origins of a word to discover its real meaning. It is said that the word display originated from the latin word "displicare" which means to open something that is folded. Examination of this explanation makes the word display easy to understand.

So, the first thing that somes to mind is that this action requires space. In other words, to carry out the act of display cannot be undertaken without space.

Secondly, the word display means to reveal the inside of something, or more specifically to carry out the verb to show. This is how the word "show" as a noun is often used to replace the word display. The reason for the invention of this second word "show" probably stems from the strong desire to make something known. This desire comes from the initial existence of information. In other words, the word display cannot exist without information.

Additionally, the meaning of display also contains the need to seek a certain reaction from those who view it. This need can only be obtained by the production of something that catches the attention of prospective viewers, which means that a display also needs the act of production.

Space, information, production. These three words become apparent when studying the origins of the word display.

What is an exhibition?

In Japanese, the word display is "tenji". It is also necessary to study the origins of the word tenji to discover more about the word display. This word is written in two chinese characters, the first of which also has the meaning of the verb to spread. The second character means to place on top of a desk or table. Placed together the obvious meaning of the word is to spread out on view on a table. In order to carry out this action once again it is necessary to have space. The strong desire to show something to others is very evident in this action. And, of course, there is also the need to receive a reaction from those who view it. In the same way as the latin translation, the Japanese word also has strong connections to the three words space, information and production. With the above explanation it was my desire to make clear from the start the meaning of the word "display".

The aim of displays.

The act of supplying information demands in return a reaction from the receiver. The required reaction is some form of motion to indicate that the viewer has absorbed the information available. This indicates that a display demands such movements in order to be successful.

The movement demanded by a display will differ in style in accordance to its location and available information. In the business world, the desired motion from the receiver is the act of purchase. In the art and museum world, the desired effect is open appreciation and prolonged study. For festivals the overall wish is for crowd-forming motions. Displays of rank demand respect and subordination. Computer and calculator displays must have accuracy on the part of the operator. In the animal world a display of emotion during courtship requests in return affection, and in times of danger it demands that the opponent respects superiority and retreats. In this way, any form of display must in return have its equal reaction. It is necessary to make the above points clear from the beginning in order to have complete understanding of the word display.

Characteristics of displays.

Displays have several varying characteristics. These characteristics depends on the form of the media available. I will therefore now point out the characteristics that are common in displays.

The affect on the five senses.

Humans are in possession of five senses. These are sight, smell, hearing, taste, touch. In addition we spend our whole life surrounded by space. If this space is utilized by the media it provides a convenient vehicle to appeal to the five senses. The reason for this is that three of the senses. The reason for this is that three of the senses, sight, touch and taste, exist within the medium of space in a tangible fashion, and the remaining two senses, hearing and smell, are transmitted through space in a less tangible way.

Participation.

Displays have their place. This means that they can openly expect the active participation of people. The act of participation is a voluntary gesture that announces a desire to gain information. Under these conditions it is necessary to provide the information with as little bother to the participant as is possible.

Upon receiving the information that this required, the participant will then offer his reaction in the form of asking questions. In accordance to the questions that the participant asks gives the displayer the opportunity to grasp his needs. In other words, there is an active flow of feed back information.

Furthermore, participation in a display also is an able opportunity to gain experience. Owing to the visual properties of a display, the experience gained tends to leave a stronger impression.

Proximity of objects.

Displays offer the participant a completely visual stimulated by the existence of displays. This means that the viewer is in extremely close proximity to the object on offer. Under these circumstances it is very easy to get across the information required. The most important element of this close proximity is the easy way in which communication can be established. It is well known that an event occuring in ones nearby proximity leaves a stronger impression than something that is learnt through hearsay.

Human intervention.

At the display area there are many cases that receive human intervention. For example, at business display places there are salesmen, and at art galleries or museums there are curators who will give explanations. These people are there to emphasize certain points or offer supplementary information. In these situations a feeling of warm trust is quite easily experienced as further information is offered by word of mouth.

Fixed display areas.

There are many areas of display which are fixed. These places seem to suffer from a weakness from the media point of view, but this is not true. The phrase "between us and the door-post" is often heard and in fact this approach sometimes has a stronger selling point than mass-communication. The existance of this phrase lends strength to this belief. To put it another way, power can be gained from any situation depending on how it is used.

The last place of the media.

There are many activities that are designed to get information across to another source. For example, in the business world there are such things as advertisements, direct mail and publicity. However, in the final stage of selling the last action that decides a successful sale is the act of display. This mean that in the end the final display relies heavily on previous activities. This reliance stems from the early input of information into a prospective purchaser's mind.

However, displays on their own also have the ability to combine all of the early stages of the process in one place. On the other hand, pre-information without the final display as a selling point is in itself very weak.

As has been mentioned above, there are many positive characteristics that the media can utilize in these displays. These characteristics must be learnt one-by-one and be utilized accordingly as they are the most important keys to the outcome of a successful display.

2) SPACE

The word place is often used instead of the word space. To describe ones home we use the phrase "my place" and the working area is most commonly known as the work-place. The word "place" summons up two distinct meanings; one which indicates space itself and the other which describes how the space has been used. Displays are connected to both meanings. In the following it is more appropriate to use the word place than it is to use the word space.

There are many places in our immediate vicinity. There are places to live, places of learning, places of enjoyment. Displays can be found in all of these places. However, the most important place of all is the place where business is carried out.

Place of business.

The business world can be separated into three different sections; places where food and beverages are served, service and after-service centers and places that sell goods. Of these three areas, the one that demands the most out of displays are places that sell goods. Owing to this, most of the following comments are in relation to this area.

Places that offer goods for sale are usually known as shops, and within shops there are two important factors. The Chinese character for the word "shop" means to show, and this sums up the first factor. This factor is strongly related to the principle aim of shops, which is to transfer the goods between the retailer and the consumer at the highest rate of turnover possible.

In Japanese another word for shop is "tana" which means shelves. This describes the ability of a shop to display many objects. This of course sums up the idea of closing the gap between the retailer and the consumer.

The main job of the display in the above is obvious in its aim; to show off as many products as is possible. The object of the display here can also be divided into two.

One is to provide a medium where the consumer is in a position to actually pick up the product which is made possible by the effective utilization of space. This is known as a token display.

The second one is the effective categorization of the products which makes for easy analyzation by the consumer by comparison. This is known as a assortment display.

However, in most cases in the business world, the type of display that is most refered to is the token display.

This token display can be found in two typical locations. One is the show-window whose main job is to sell to people have have not yet entered the shop, and the second is the display that is found within the shop which is known as show-space. I will now give further details on these two places in the following.

Show-windows.

Show-windows are often called the face of a shop. This name in itself describes the importance of this type of display. I suppose the face of a human-being is equally important, which really sums up just how invaluable a show-window is to a shop. Without doubt the show-window is the first impression that a prospective consumer has of the shop and should therefore be conspicuous. It is the place where the eyes are first drawn. It is therefore natural that it has great importance.

So, in general what is the exact level of importance that the show-window has?

Ability of transfering information.

The basic ability of a show-window lays within the ease in which it can transfer information. Using this medium the type of information that can be got across is the type of products available, the style of the shop, the period, the main attractions and life-style. As the show-window is the most conspicuous part of this shop, its first-impression value is great.

Attracting the correct consumer.

The show-window is used to attract the eyes of the people passing by, and according to the style of the display it is effective in sorting out the style of consumer that the shop wishes to attract. The division of these two factors is dependant on the main character of the shop. It should have the ability to attract any passer-by on the assumption that he will purchase something, and also has the ability to attract only the type of consumer who is more likely to purchase some form of specialized product.

Factor of selling the products.

Shops are intended to sell as many products as they can. Also it is a place that people can see the products on display even after the shop has closed. So, this is a big factor in enticing people back to the shop. The word window-shopping expresses this factory very well.

The treatment of the consumer.

Treatment of the consumer is also important in the shop. Treatment in this case means the way in which respect and kindness are shown to the customer and the way in which one responds to the customers' interest. This is a place where expression comes easy. Also, the attitude in its approach to consumers can easily be changed. Owing to this the expression of a shop can alternate in accordance to the needs of the market.

Topic construction.

Elaborate expression draws the interest of prospective consumers. This becomes the topics of peoples conversation. These topics are then spread further through the vehicle of the media. This therefore becomes an open advertisement for the shop. If a shop is not the topic the conversation, it is necessary to bring its ability into full play to ensure that it becomes one.

The creation of the town scene.

Shops are in general aimed towards the market-place of towns and cities. Shopping is made easy in the town as the show-windows are linked together in very close proximity to each other. This means that the visual scene of the town is created by the existence of the shops. Shops, in turn, are dependant on these towns and cities. Within this dependance it is also the duty of the shops to contribute to the needs of the town. Within this responsibility in mind, it is the duty of shops to create the scenery of the towns by use of their displays.

In this way show-windows have a large job to perform in the towns. With the differing factors mentioned above, the shop has to choose which one it will concentrate its efforts on, and the final decision is usually based on the character of the shop, the location, the size of the show-window, shape and the period. In order to make a successful display, all of the above points must be studied and taken into careful consideration. A display that does not match the surrounding environment and available market cannot expect good results.

Show space.

Show space is an area within the shop that can be used effectively for sales and is known under different names according to the shop; VP space, show area, magnet, focus point, etc., etc.

Also, depending on the shape of the shop there are different types of show space; on the floor, on the wall, hanging from the ceiling, etc. These show spaces can take several different forms; stages, tables, shelves, panels, glass-cases, wagons, etc. So, what is the main use for these show spaces?

Ability of pointing out direction of products.

Most of the questions received from customers in shops are in connection with the location of goods. To save the salesman wasting time answering such questions, it is necessary to have some form of indication within the shop of where the products are. The most saleable items should therefore be placed in the most prominent place.

3) INFORMATION

Ability to get across the character of the shop.

Shops are in a position to show their unique character to their customers. The shop must show its character to the customers in order to exist. It is therefore the role of the shop to ensure that its customers are in full possession of the details. The shop uses its displays to get this information over to the consumer and therein draws out the desire to purchase a product.

The ability to explain the products.

All shops have specific products which they would like to sell. For example, these would be new products on the market. Of course the shop must give a clear explanation of the product to the prospective purchaser; the device itself, its function and capability, how to use it, how to put it to use, the material from which it has been made, the place where it has been made, method of production and any other general information. This display will additionally indicate trends in present-day living standards.

Ability to display main attractions.

All shops have the need to urge sales onto the consumer by offering special attractions. Displays take a large part in getting the information of the attraction acorss to the public. Also, the display gives the chance to improve the attractiveness of the product to make it more easily saleable, and this is one of its most important roles.

The ability to produce a degree of freshness.

One of the more convenient roles of the display is in the fact that it can be easily altered. With this ability the display can keep a constant feeling of freshness within the shop. The impression of the display left on the customers relates directly to the surrounding parts of the shop.

The ability to add color and flavor to the shop.

According to the brightness and inspiration of the display, a touch of bustling color can be added to the overall atmosphere of the shop. This is not in order to increase the personal feeling of the customer, but in order to create an atmosphere where people will gather freely. These people in their turn will also add to the color and flavor of the shop.

Treatment of customers.

A shop is a place directed at consumers. Customers must be drawn to the shop. Displays have the ability to do this. In the same way as a show-window, the clients desire to be in the shop is increased by elaborate displays.

Customer movement.

Choosing the place to put displays carefully is an effective means of urging the customers to move around the shop. This gives the customer the opportunity to see as many of the shops products as possible. But this is not all. Movement puts the customer in mood of positivity and this translated into action. The main purpose of displays is to encourage the customers into positive action, so this function must not be overlooked.

What is information?

We are now in what in known as the age of information. Because of this there is more and more interest focused on the collection of information.

So, what exactly is information?

The Japanese characters for the word information means "mind" for the first character and "news" for the second. In conjunction with each other it is obvious that the meaning is new that stimulates the minds of people.

So, at what time do peoples' minds gain this stimulation? It is when the person receiving information immediately recognizes it as useful.

So what is this feeling of stimulation like? It is a feeling of satisfaction that the information has met ones demands.

Which means that news alone does not meet the category of information. However, it is one of the tools that lead one down the path of information.

Information materials.

Firstly, the materials of information must be gathered together. There are many varying materials available at the place of work. These materials come in the form of products, periods, shops themselves, main attractions and life-styles. Amongst these materials let us examine what we have.

Information materials for products.

Products have many effects. If can be said that these are the materials for information. This source can be divided into two the effective result following use and the symbol, the object itself.

1) Effective end result

This end result is the main aim of production and incorporates into its structure ease of use, safe usage and personal satisfaction to the user. The factors that produce this end result are clear explanations of use, functions, capability, materials, quality, colour, size, shape, method of production, the time when it should be used, the place of use, the opportunity of use and the main objective for which it was made.

2) Symbolistic result

The end result being a symbol, is when instead putting the object to use it is used to show to others for personal satisfaction. The characterization of these symbols usually comes from objects such as brand names, makers, authors, place of production, atmosphere, style, origin, etc., etc.

Whether a shop makes its own products or collects them from other sources, the intention of stocking the products is clear. This intention is decided by the area of sales that the shop wishes to emphasize. This point must be made clear before the stocking process is undertaken.

The information available for the period.

It is the duty of the shop to stock products that match the period. The present period plays a big part in all of our daily lives. Information becomes available from the period. Let us now examine the importance that shops play in our daily lives within a certain period.

1) Ceremonial periods.

Seasonal ceremonies, social ceremonies, local ceremonies, national ceremonies, family ceremonies, etc.

2) Celebrational periods.

After recovery, birth, school entrance, graduation, coming of age, long life, house-warming, receiving awards, etc.

3) Periods of expressions of sympathy.

During hot weather, cold weather, after a fire, visits to hospital, etc.

4) Gift periods.

New year, mid-summer, year-end, Christmas, etc.

5) Periods of receiving goods.

Receiving a fresh supply of goods, receipt of regular goods, etc.

6) Purchase periods.

This is an origin to all periods or occasions. There are many points within these origins that are able to draw ones attention. Owing to this they must also therefore be considered as a medium for information.

Information materials in relation to shops.

The general form of shopping is such that one will choose a shop before choosing the item one wishes to buy. It is therefore necessary to collect information about several shops before going shopping. In order to gain this information, the following points must be taken into consideration.

1) The environment of the shop.

Place, building, interiod, etc.

2) The characteristics of the shop.

Days of opening, opening hours, goods on sale, price of the goods available, is the shop representative of its kind, the type of customers, the shop attracts, the history, etc.

3) The service available.

Packaging service, delivery service in relation to other shops, free gift service, etc.

It is now very necessary for all shops to have a very distinct individuality. The reason for this is that the consumers have unique life-styles and demand products and services that fit into these life-styles.

Information on main attractions,

All shops have many main attractions. The main aim of these attractions is to urge the customer into purchasing the product. To do this the spread of information is most important to have people flock to the shop and create an atmosphere congenial to the purchase of many products. The materials needed to get this information across are as follows:

1) Information on contents such as style and purpose of the product.

2) Information on when the product is available.

3) Information on the place and scale of the attraction.

Information in relation to life-styles.

All shops have to direct their aims towards the life-styles of the customers. They must play a role to offer guidance to the continued flow of changing life-styles. In order to do this they must be in possession of information that is related to modern life-styles. The following pieces are what is needed to do this; a knowledge of politics, the economy, history, movements abroad, etc. Everything surrounding us has an effect on our daily lives. In order to gather this information it is necessary to extend our antennas as wide as possible. Information must be gathered while it is still new.

Gathering information.

There are many pieces of information to be gathered in business. In order to gather in this information, one must have a base to start from. One of the bases that is best to work from is the demands of the public, as was mentioned earlier on. These demands vary from person-to-person, so the most essential things are as follows:

The origins of instinct.

Personal expression.

The distinction between others.

Things that bring happiness.

Things that stimulate the mind and soul.

Provides a rich knowledge.

Things that satisfy curiosity.

Things that bring out peoples possessiveness.

The above of course depends on the environment and the age group of the consumers. It is important to remember these things.

The next point is to investigate the fine points of these demands and grasp firm hand on the next step. The most common idea would be to grasp an idea that is already popular with the public. In short, the research into popularity of products has already proved its worth. Magazines, television programmes and film scenes serve as a good reference for this. These media points have already been proved to be in the minds of the public. It is well-known that people draw scenes in their minds as to exactly what they want.

The motive of the purchase is another origin for the search for information. This means that people buy things for different reasons. This motivations stems from many varying areas, such as good quality; the product is fashionable; because it has a long life; as a gift.

The type of customers the shop wishes to attract is known as the target. It is therefore necessary for the shop to study the characteristics of their own individual target. The demands differ according to the target.

A further point for the collection of information depends on the local competition, the local area and the timing.

If this information and these materials are combined and filtered to match the type of shop that is being planned, then this means the collection of information has been successful.

There is also a feeling of existence. There are both people and things that simply cannot be ignored and the word "existence" is a good word to describe them.

People and things that cannot be ignored means that they have effected you in a certain way. Separating them like this is another means of gaining information. If this is correct, shops, building and displays all have this feeling of existence and therefore cannot be ignored.

The things that the creation of information makes.

Shops give off a great aura of information. People take in this information and when they have accumulated enough they will know enough about the shop. That is known as "image". This image has the great power to change peoples' intentions, so the strength of the shop must be considered very seriously. If the accumulation of information creates images, it is possible to operate image through the operation of information. Therefore, it is very important to give the shop the correct image and in doing so filter out the information that does not fit the imge. Recently the word C. I. (Corporate Identity) is becoming popular as it concentrates on the detail available and therefore products an image.

This means that a display must also have a desirable image and all efforts must be put into ensuring this aim.

4) PRODUCTION

Production means to produce and expression. With this in mind it is easy to imagine that displays in the place of business command the services of equipment, goods, lighting, properties and sounds. Fragrance could also be added to this list. And, of course, there is also the demand for the appearance of humans.

Then, what in fact does it express?

One thing is the creation of an excited feeling. The second is to express the formulation of concrete information.

To what is needed to create a feeling of excitement?

Enjoyment.

Enjoyment comes before anything else. One of the basic of delight is the stimulation of the eyes. For example, something could be shiny, bright and colourful, offer interesting motion, be plentiful, be of an unusual shape, and so on.

Writing stories is one of the ways of creating enjoyment. In this light it is obvious that a medium for creating dream-like fantasies is full of enjoyment.

And also show business is a treasure-trove of emjoyment. Especially the stars who visually take an active part in show business. Clowns play the most important part of all. Clowns have the ability to replace displays with their attention-drawing factors.

Besides these things there are many more things in our daily life from which we can draw enjoyment; such as the world of sports, festivals, eroticism and nostalgia.

However, it is also necessary to bring unexpected to this enjoyment to increase its value. The meaning of unexpected is some kind of combination that has the ability to shock the viewer in the same way that an unexpected twist to a story has. The enjoyment of magic and trickery are created by this combination of the unexpected.

It is imperative that this enjoyment is not missed in order to get the information across. Many types of information will miss their target if they are not wrapped in pretty paper and labeled "enjoyment". After all, enjoyment plays the most important role of all in the world of displays.

Friendliness.

When friendliness is experienced it has the ability the excite the soul of the receiver. Such friendliness usually has its roots in sympathy. It seems as if humans offer sympathy on a system of supply and demand. This emotion is felt on such occasions as when an interesting object is offered for comment, and piece of unusual information is passed across and when a covered object is presented in gift-form.

With this is mind it is necessary to choose as a main item for a display something that will incite the feeling of sympathy in the beholder. Certain kinds of events, news and seasonal impressions are the very things. Anything that is close to the core of human emotions is guaranteed to effective. This is, of course, quite natural considering that we are all human beings.

The expression of popular atmosphere and the image of the age are excellent for the purpose of winning sympathy. This goes to proove that elements of fashion and modern art technology are suitable objects to guage the feeling of the present age.

This friendliness must also be evident in order to get across information. The information that people receive from those closest to them is accepted with little difficulty. Now it is easy to understand why friendliness is so important.

Beauty.

Beauty which excites the soul must also never be forgotten. But beauty is a difficult concept to grasp clearly as it is based on subjectivity. However, it is well known that there is a kind of common beauty that can be acknowledged by everyone.

An explanation of true meaning of beauty has been attempted by many scholars. Words such as "discipline", "unity" and their opposites "complexity" and "alteration" have all appeared in these theories. Perhaps the meanings of these words should be related to their own sense of beauty.

The meaning of the words "discipline" and "unity" is to put things in order; to arrange and repeat; to systematize and balance. The meaning of the words "complexity" and "alteration" is to move; to compare and to emphasize.

By combining these opposites together, a sense of beauty could easily be created. For example, beauty is created by uniting movement to something balanced.

High quality.

A combination of beauty and quality has the ability to produce and even higher quality. This combination also contains a factor that can stimulate ones emotions.

Then how is quality measured?

It is perhaps somethings that has been produced by a favorable situation, by wisdom and by the hands of many people who understand the sensitivity of others.

After all, wisdom, care and sensitivity are all essential ingredients to ensure that people become excited.

A description of hospitality

It is possible to paraphrase the above explanations and change the destination of the meaning to that of a description of hospitality. This is because hospitality is the art of expressing good-will and respect. It is all linked with enjoyment, friendliness beauty and high quality.

A place of business is also a place where guests are received. The act of hospitality certainly cannot be overlooked there. In this way hospitality also plays a very important role.

In order to get information across

In display work it is important to not only make the information easily understandable, but at the same time to think about the expression of the information. Various techniques can be used to this end. Let me explain a few of these.

The eye catcher.

It is foremostly important to catch peoples' eyes in order to get the information across. To do this it is necessary to employ certain tricks. These are called eye-catchers or attention games. They could be called things that attract the attention of the eyes. Such things should be stimulative lights which shine brightly, things that have motion, bright colors, stimulating shapes, unusual objects, the unexpected, strange combinations, etc.

Such are the elements that produce enjoyment. Which goes to proove that enjoyment goes hand in hand with the meaning of eye-catchers.

Attraction.

This is the means to draw peoples' attention to displays. Therefore, the way to easily attract the attention of the eye should be carefully thought about. Plain layouts which do not confuse the eye, lighting and backgrounds should respect much consideration.

Sometimes products are made with the sole idea in mind of attracting peoples' attention. This is owing to the fact that the initial tactile impression is very necessary to concentrate the consciousness.

Also, it is very necessary to rid the background of complicated distractions. Such obstructions can only make the attention wander. This especially applies to shops which have to offer for sale an assortment of products and equipment. The interior of these such must look tidy.

Fresh impressions.

The very existence of information relies on its freshness. Owing to this the public demand to be impressed with new information. Changing the basic appearance of the information available in order to make it seem new is very important. There are various elements available to effect this change, such as revised layouts, backgrounds, alteration of color schemes, equipment, interior design and combinations of the stock. However, much thought must be given to the change as a change for the same or worse will obviously not have any effect at all. Another way is to make the products stand out. New products should be emphasized with a signboard or show-card.

It is a good idea to maintain a good knowledge of the news and latest topics. In such cases the swiftness of response becomes important; things should immediately be altered according to the change in demands.

Clarity.

Displays rely on the brief moment that the consumer passes by. This is why simplicity and clarity take on a large importance. People in general dislike complications. Especially now that the times are becoming more and more busy; the busier we get, the less we like complications.

Having a good idea of the clarity with which you wish to get the information across is necessary in order to create a simple display. If you cannot understand the main message of the display yourself, you can expect nothing more from the consumer. It is also necessary to gather up the information that is needed and focus it clearly. Most people find it difficult to take in a lot of separate stimulation at the same time.

Another point is to put things down in writing. The written word is all powerful in the sense that it has a definate meaning and give across a feeling of reliability. It is a good idea to sum up the main point in as few words as possible and then ensure that the writing is attractive.

The creation of atmosphere.

This is the art of giving the viewer the impression of being in an actual situation. In the world of displays this can be achieved by settling the scenery. This method has great effects. Products will get across their own ability to the best effect by being seen in use. At the same time it offers a form on education as to use the instrument.

But this is not the sole reason. Humans have the ability to create sceneries within their own heads. As people tend to keep strong impressions within their minds, nothing is more stimulating than a good visual display.

Additionally, having seen the display one automatically has the feeling that an extra experience has been gained. Although it is a false experience, the seed of stimulation has undoubtedly been planted. Such things leave a strong impression.

Planning and effective combination.

This is the art of achieving the best results by using the combination of two powers. Displays are flexible enough to be able to bring their full ability into full play at the drop of a hat. This is one of the original characteristics of displays which concentrate the last stage of the act onto the act of actual purchase.

Besides the display itself, a complete knowledge of the expression needed to make the information effective is demanded for good results. The actual usage should also be concentrated upon. For example, if advertisement are used, then the same characters symbols and slogans must be used on the display. By doing this people are reminded of the advertisement and of half the job of the display is already completed. People tend to forget most of the things that they are have seen previously, so if the opportunity presents itself it is good to add a little stimulation to the memory in order to jog the mind. Even if the stimuli is absorbed and the viewer moves on without action, a good result can be expected in the long run.

第5章　演出の材料

ディスプレイの材料の中で，人間ほど優れたものはありません。人間が最も興味をもつものは人間だからです。これは，あらゆるメディアが証明しています。街に貼られたポスター，テレビのコマーシャル，雑誌の表紙など，それぞれに人間の活躍が目につきます。この世の中は，人間が中心の世の中，人間に興味があつまるのは当然のことでしょう。

そこで，ディスプレイの場でも，いろいろな人間が活躍するのです。その人間の代表格は見世物の世界の人間達。楽しさを提供することが仕事ですから，これも当然でしょう。

❶❷❸❹

この人間達の中でも，とくに目立つのが道化師。この道化師にもいろいろな種類があります。ここに登場しているのはピエロ。フランスのパントマイムの道化役ですが，大変になじみの深いもの，それだけに使いやすい材料といっていいでしょう。

❶

5)MATERIALS FOR PRODUCTION

HUMANS

There is no better theme for displays than humans. This is owing to the fact that us humans find nothing more interesting than others of the same species. This is prooved by every category of the media. The activities of humans can be seen on posters plastered around town, on television commercials, in magazines, etc., etc. This world is based on humans so it is natural for us to be attracted.

This is why so many humans take an active part in displays. The most typical area of this type of human display is the world of entertainment. This is also quite natural considering their main job is to keep us amused and provide us with enjoyment.

❶❷❸❹

The people who stand out most as entertainers are the clowns. These come in many different forms. There are the pierots who dominate the art of mime in France, and owing to their amiable character they are probably the easiest to handle.

❷

❸

❹

❺❻

フールと呼ばれるものもいます。その名が
示している通り愚かさを売物にする道化師。
だんだらの服，金ピカの飾り，鈴，ロバの耳
と角のついた帽子，しっぽ，といったものが，
この道化師の伝統的なスタイルです。このス
タイル，いろいろなものに利用できそうです。

❼

ここに登場しているのはパントマイマー。
この芸人は，身体で語りかけることが仕事で
すから，ものを言えないマネキンも，この役
にすれば優れた語り手になるでしょう。

❺

❺❻

*There are clowns which resemble the village
idiot. As can be gathered from the name they
specialize in totally foolish acts. The traditional
costumes of clowns utilize checked clothing,
glitter, bells, hats with donkeys' ears, horns and
tails. These styles can be used in many different
situations.*

❼

*The clown here is a mime-artist. His job is
to talk by using his body which means that a
person afflicted with a speech impediment could
be a perfect story-teller by mastering this art.*

❻

❼

❽❾❿

ダンサー達はディスプレイの世界でもスターです。身についた華やかさと動きをのある肢体が，ディスプレイを盛りあげるからです。そして，この人間達が発散するエロティシズムも見逃せません。

❽❾❿

Dancers are also stars in the world of displays. This is because a limb which naturally give off an aura of exquisite movement lends itself automatically to the basic idea of display. The erotisism exuded by these people is something that just cannot be ignored.

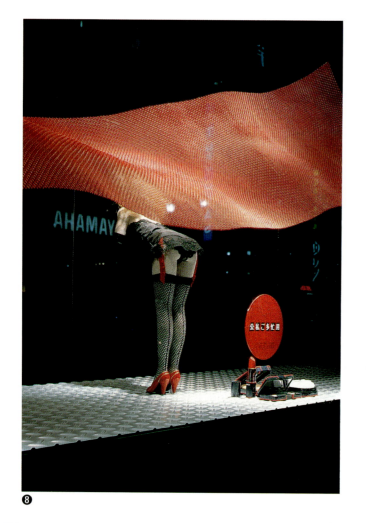

❽

❿

9

⓫

サンドイッチマンも見世物の世界の人間、近頃は、あまり見られなくなりましたが、これは道路事情のせい。ディスプレイの場に復活させたい人間の一人です。もともと情報を伝えることが仕事ですから、ディスプレイの世界でも大きな働きをするでしょう。

⓬ ⓭

盗賊や囚人といった裏街道の人間達も登場させたいものの一つ。普段、街中では目にすることのできない人間達だけに、見世物になることは確かでしょう。このスキャンダラスな人間達を、いかに洗練させてみせるかが腕のみせ所です。

⓫

Also, sandwich-board men also belong to the world of entertainment. The reason why these people are disappearing from our everyday life can be put down to the present condition of the roads. These people should be put to active use in the display areas. As the main purpose of their job is to pass on information, their contribution could be huge.

⓬ ⓭

The visual aspect of those people who inhabit the backstreets of life such as burglers and prisoners are also desperately needed for displays. As they are not the type of people who can regularly be seen around the town they are definately something not to be missed. The method of how to make these scandalous people retain an aspect of refinery is up to your own skill.

⓫

⑫

⑬

❶❷

顔を隠すことは，興味を起こさせるための効果的な方法です。隠されたものに対しては，誰もが興味を示しますから。

また，人間の顔は大変に強い性格をもっています。それだけに，ディスプレイの雰囲気を左右します。そこで，時には顔を隠す必要もでてくるのです。

❶❷

Hiding the face is one way to stimulate peoples' interest. This is because most people have a distinct tendancy to show an interest towards things that are hidden.

This fact is compounded by the the strong character contained within the face. It will automatically influence the display, so it is sometimes necessary to hide the face.

❶

❷

❸

人間の後姿にも興味をそそられます。その人間の向う側を意識するためでしょうか、それとも、無視されることへの反発でしょうか。

この後姿が人垣になると、効果はさらに高まります。人垣をかき分けて、向う側が見たいという衝動は、誰もがもつでしょう。そして、この方法、空間の奥行を広く感じさせる効用もあるようです。

❸

A back view of a person also has the ability to stimulate peoples' interest. Could this be because we are all slightly conscious of the darker side of each others' nature or because we are a little outraged at being ignored so blatantly?

A rear view of a crowd is even better. The natural instict in anybody is to elbow their way through to see what they are missing. This method also has the added ability to make the depth of available space seem wider.

❸

❹❺

　人間が身を飾ることのすべては，人の関心を呼ぶための仕掛です。この優れた仕掛を利用しない手はないでしょう。化粧，刺青，髭，ボディペインティング，衣裳，装身具，いろいろな仕掛があります。

　このディスプレイに使われている仕掛は，ボディペインティング。人があつまって，一つの南国情景になっているところが面白さを際立てています。

❹❺

The only reason that people like to dress up is in order to draw attention to themselves. This excellent technique must be taken advantage of. There are many available evenues to concentrate upon; make-up, tatoos, hair, moustaches, body-painting, costumes, accessories, etc.

The technique used in this display is body-painting. A crowd of people making up a view of the South is truly remarkable.

❹

❺

❶❷❸

人の気配とは，人間が居ると察せられる状況をつくることです。例えばこのディスプレイのように，手先だけで人の存在を表わす方法があります。この方法は，人間を表立って使うよりも印象を強くすることができるのです。隠されていることによって印象が強くなるからでしょう。そして，想像するものは現実のものよりも魅力的です。

この状況づくりには，さらに，人影を見せる方法，足跡や手形を見せる方法，飲みかけのグラスや喫いさしの煙草，読みかけの本といった小道具を使う方法など，いろいろなことが考えられます。

APPEARENCE OF PEOPLE

❶❷❸

The appearence of people is a means of creating a situation which subtly hints at the existence of others. For example, as shown in this display the existence of other people is indicated by the mere appearance of fingers. This method can produce a stronger impression than using a complete view of somebody. This is owing to the fact that something hidden from view causes more interest. Imagination is always more attractive than real life.

There are many methods that can be utilized to hint at the existence of people such a hand or foot prints, an empty glass, a half-smoked cigarette, a half-read book, etc.

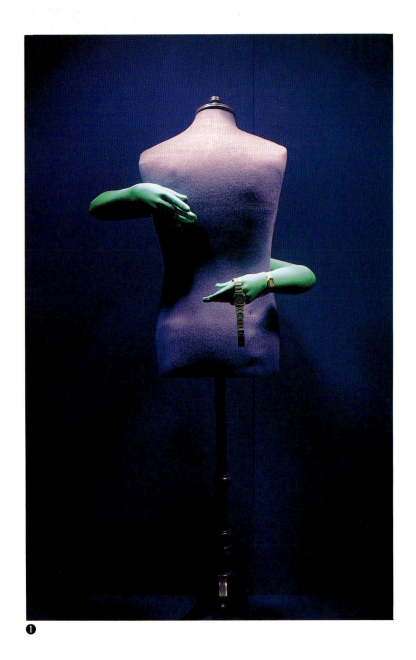

❶

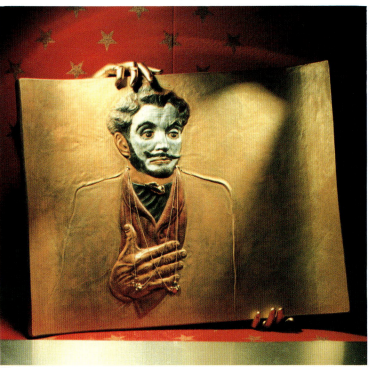

❷

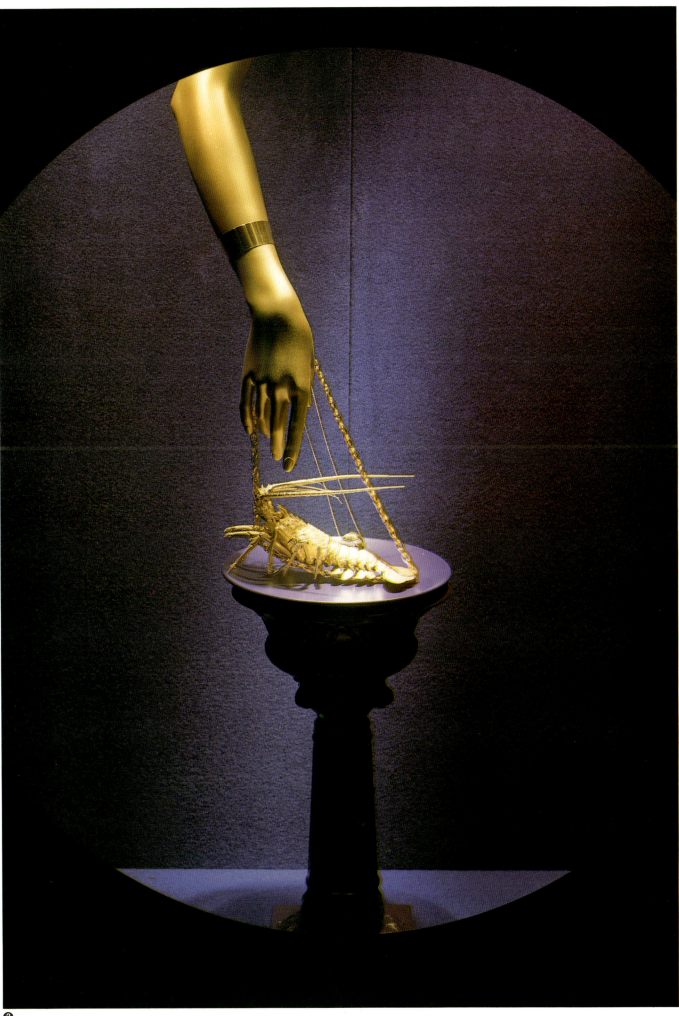

人形 　　　　　　　　　　　　　DOLLS

❶❷❸❹

　人形もディスプレイの世界で活躍します。現実の世界から幻想の世界まで，そして，小さな世界から大きな世界まで，いろいろな世界がつくり出せるからです。

　見世物の世界での活躍の歴史も見逃せません。それぞれの国に，歴史をもった人形劇があります。その歴史が，人形劇に楽しさのイメージを与えたのです。

　さらに，この人形に対する思い入れには，大変に大きなものがあります。信仰や願望のさいの身代わりの役を果たしてきたからでしょう。また，子供の頃から長い間，遊びの対象として慣れ親しんできたことも見逃せません。

❶❷❸❹

Dolls can also play a large part in the world of the display. This creates the idea that many different worlds can be available from the real world to fantasy worlds and from small worlds to large worlds.

And, of course, the world of show-business must not be overlooked. Every country has its own popular puppet shows which have their roots in that particular country's history. This prevalent image of history gives a delightful touch to the puppet shows.

Furthermore, the tendency towards deep meditation on these dolls by humans plays a big role. It is considered that this rises from the role that varrious types of dolls have had in our previous life in religion and personal wishes. Additionally the fact that we have grown so familar with dolls ever since our youth lends strength to this meditation.

❶

②

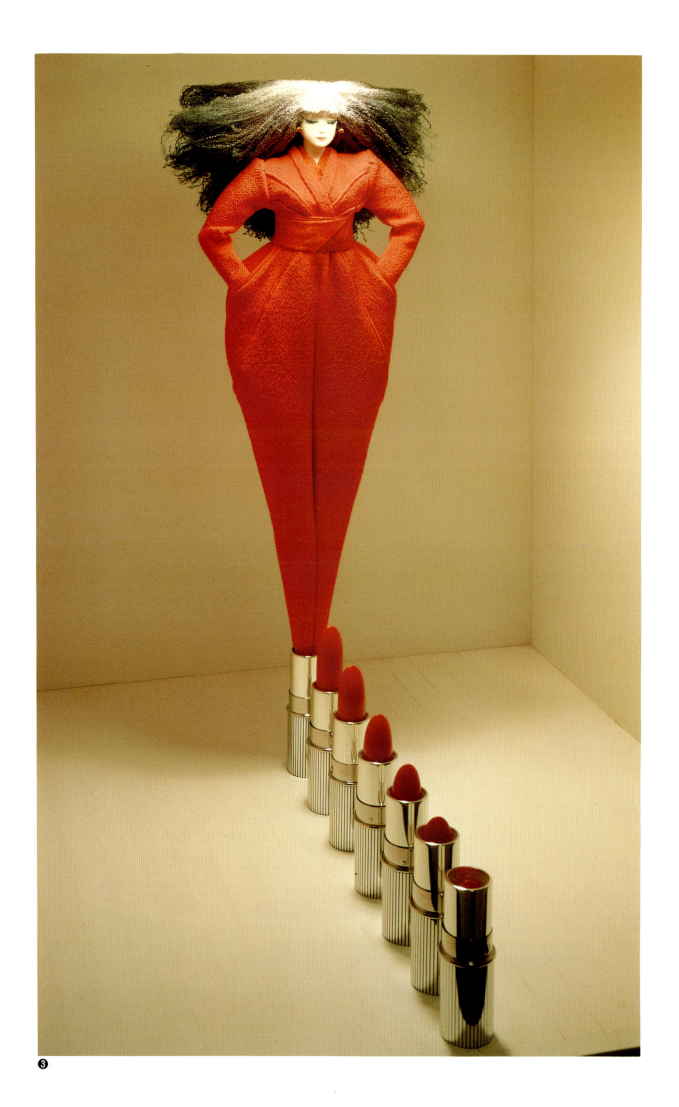

❸

36

4

仮面の魅力は，大変に大きなものです。その魅力は，仮面がもっている不思議な力から生まれてくるのでしょう。なにしろ，祭りの場で，これを付けた人間が所作をすると，周囲の人はエクスタシーに陥りやすいといわれていますから。また，これを付けると人間が変わるともいわれています。この優れた力を利用しない手はないでしょう。

❶

仮面は，性格を誇張して表わす力をもっています。また，象徴的に表わす力もあります。そこから，いろいろな使い道が生まれてきます。この世界時計もその一つ。仮面に描かれた国旗のパターンが，それぞれの国を表わしています。

❷

顔を隠すことは，秘密めいた雰囲気をつくり出します。そして，そこから刺激的な物語が生まれるのです。ここに登場しているマネキンも，仮面をつけることによって，劇的なヒロインになっているようです。

MASKS

Masks have great charm. This charm seems to be produced from the uncanny power that masks seem to possess. Whatever this power is, it is a wellknown fact that a masked face appearing at festivals can give the atmosphere a feeling of ecstasy. It is also said that people change their character when wearing masks. It would be a waste indeed if this incredible power was not used.

❶

Masks have the power to exaggerate the characteristics of people. They also have the power to express symbolism. The widest use of masks can be put down to these powers. This world clock is one of them; the flag patterns on the mask indicates each country.

❷

The act of covering the face creates an atmosphere of secrecy. The ideas for many exciting stories have been founded behind this idea. The manekin that appears here seems somehow heroic simply by wearing a mask.

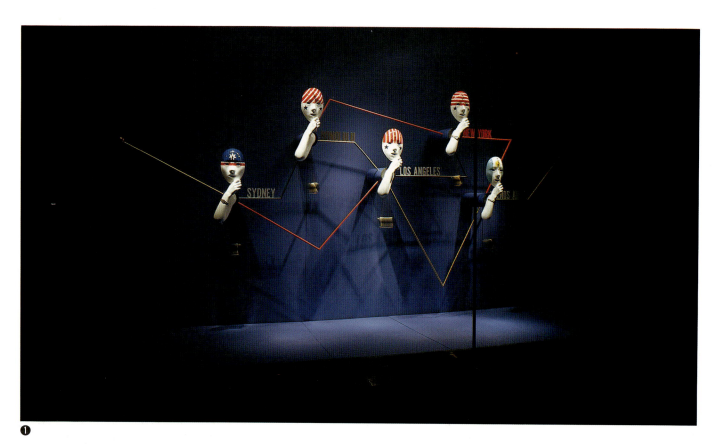

❶

❷

❸

　仮面舞踏会では，そこで行われたことは人格とは無関係と見なすという暗黙の了解があるそうです。それが，この舞踏会を特別に楽しいものにしているのでしょう。この楽しさは，ディスプレイでも表現したいものの一つです。

❹

　仮面には華やいだ雰囲気があります。祭りとの結びつきが生み出すものでしょう。このディスプレイが，その性格を示しています。また，ここでは，手と仮面だけで人の存在を表わしています。このような象徴的な表現は，ディスプレイに欠かせないもの，過剰な説明は印象を弱くするからです。

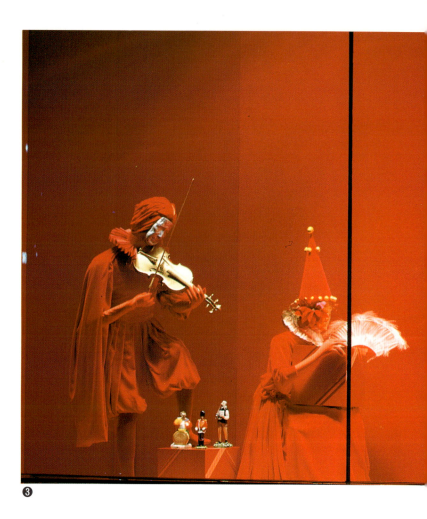

❸

❸

There is said to be in the world of fancy-dress the tacit consent that people's behavior must have no connection at all with their real character. This seemingly makes the party more enjoyable. Such enjoyment must also be expressed within the display.

❹

Masks summon up a feeling of gaiety. This must derive from their connection with festivals. This display shows such a characteristic. The existence of a person is also indicated here by the expression of a hand and a mask. Such symbolized expression cannot be overlooked in displays as too much explanation will weaken the impression.

❹

光

すべてのものは光によって見えます。見せることを目的とするディスプレイにとって欠かすことのできないものであることは確かです。とくに，ものを際立てて見せるためには大きな力を発揮します。ハイライトと影によってものの存在感を強めて見せるからです。

光は劇を盛り上げる力をもっています。劇場では，光の演出が欠かせないものであることからもわかるでしょう。

人を呼びよせるためにも光は活躍します。誘蛾灯とか集魚灯というものがありますが，光によって呼び寄せられるのは，このような動物達だけではないのです。

❶❷
人を呼び寄せるために，とくに力を発揮するのが豆電球。この小さな輝きは，あつまって大きな働きをします。無数の豆電球に彩られた飛行船，同じく豆電球でつくり出された都会の夜景，そのきらめきの情景の華やかさは，光だけがつくり出せるものといっていいでしょう。

LIGHTING

Every on earth becomes visible in accordance to its lighting. It is not an over-statement to say that the correct use of lights must not be missed on displays. Lights have the power to emphasize the full purpose of an object by showing it in striking contrast. A real feeling of existence can be strongly pronounced by the use of light and shadow.

Lighting has the effect of creating the true atmosphere of a play and therefore plays a very important role in the theatre. Lighting is used to give the effect that a single actor or a group of actors are closer than others. There are lights that can lure all types of animals and fish, but these smaller creatures are not the only things that are attracted by light.

❶❷
Miniature bulbs show their ability in attracting people. Their twinkling can have a great effect on a group of people. The gorgeousness of an air-ship covered in numerousess bulbs and the beauty of a glittering city seen at night are created only by lights.

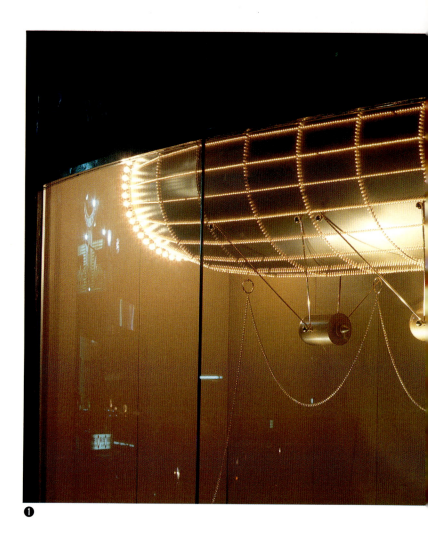

❶

❷

❸❹❺

光を見せ場に使ったディスプレイの例です。これらの効果は，周囲の明るさによって左右されますから，事前の調査が必要です。とくに太陽光の下では，すべての光は無力になりますから，昼間の顔を用意する必要があるでしょう。

❸❹❺

Here are examples of displays that utilize the power of lights. The effects are influenced by the brightness of the surroundings, so an investigation beforehand is necessary. As lights lose their power under direct sunlight it is necessary to create the face of day-time.

❸

❹

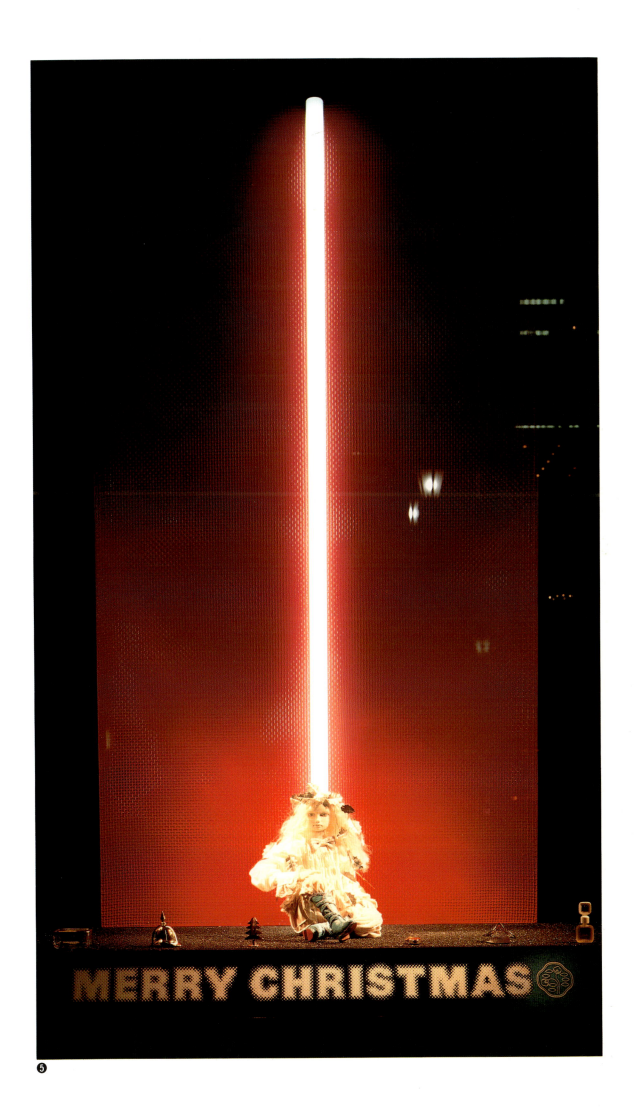

❻

劇を盛りあげる照明の中で，最も活躍するのがホリゾントライト。ものを浮びあがらせて見せるだけではありません。劇的効果を高め，空間に広がりを与える働きもするからです。人間が空を飛ぶという夢物語にぴったりの照明といっていいでしょう。

❼❽

ディスプレイとは都会の劇といっていいでしょう。その劇にふさわしい光の材料がネオンランプ，造形が自由，点滅が自在，その上輝度が高く，色も多数用意されているといった具合に大変に優れた材料です。最近は，光が管の中を走るネオンランプも活躍しています。

❻

The most commonly used lighting in the theatre is the horizontal light. This not only gives over the impression that things are floating, but also make things seems wider in a theatrical sense. This type of lighting is perfect for fantasies such as achieving the effect of a person flying.

❼❽

It would not be wrong to imply that displays are in fact urban plays. The lighting equipment suitable for displays are neon tubes. They are very easy to use with regards to the on-off switching and they are bright and come in many colors. They are excellent materials. Nowadays the world of lighting is being lived within tubes.

❻

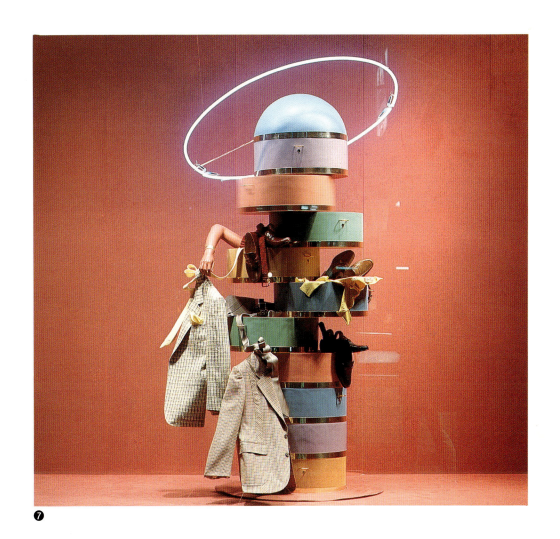

❼

❽

⑨

影も光がつくり出すものです。この影は，ものの存在を強めて見せる脇役的な存在ですが，このディスプレイのように主役になることもあります。この前で，手影絵の真似をする人もいるでしょう。このように，人をまきこみ，参加を促すディスプレイは，強い印象を与えずにはおきません。

⑨

Shadow is also created by light. Although shadow usually takes a subordinate part in displays in order to emphasize the existance of the object under harsh light, it sometimes that a leading role such as in this display. In the foreground is a person making shadow displays with his hands. In this way a display which involves people and urges their participation gives a very strong impression indeed.

⑨

❶❷❸❹

色は人の感覚に直接訴えかける力をもっています。それだけに，気分を大いに盛りあげます。その力の大きさは，ちょっと他のものには見当たりません。その力が最も大きく働くのは，この写真のように色とりどりのものをもちこんだ時，その楽しさ，華やかさは，色彩だけがつくり出せる世界といっていいでしょう。

COLORS

❶❷❸❹

Colors have the ability to appeal directly to peoples' senses. Furthermore they stimulate the inner feelings of people. No other substance has an equivalent ability. When colorful objects are introduced in this manner it shows their power to the full. The gay, gorgeous world that is the sole possession of color.

❶

❷

❸

❹

❺

　また色は，色相，明度，彩度，有彩，無彩といった属性によって，いろいろな効果を発揮します。

　その効果の一つは感情効果。色の性質によって重さと軽さ，硬さと軟かさ，暖さと寒さ，明るさと暗さ，を感じさせることができます。

　次にあげられるのは連想効果。見る人によって，多少の違いはあるものの，基本的なもので，共通して連想するものがあります。例えばこのディスプレイに使われている赤い色，この色が連想させるものは祭りや危険。この連想がクリスマスという祭りの雰囲気をもりあげています。

❻

　同じかたちを使っても，色によってこのように印象が違ってきます。ここに使われている緑色が連想させるものは調和や安全。そこで，このように落ち着いた雰囲気のディスプレイになるのです。

　さらに，色には進出色と後退色，膨張色と収縮色とがあります。暖色系の色は，進出色であり膨張色です。寒色系の色は後退色であり収縮色です。この二つのディスプレイを見較べてみるとそのことがよくわかります。

❺

❺

The various effects of colors depend on such things as shade, the extent of the brightness, the extent of the coloring, the actual coloring or the lack of coloring.

One of the effects that colors can stimulate is feeling. According to the characteristic of the color, people can feel heaviness or lightness, hardness and softness, warmth and cold, brightness and darkness.

Next comes the effect of colors on the imagination. There is a slight difference in this, however, as people tend to have a common feeling when it comes to basic colors. For example, let us study the color red which is used in this display. This color can either indicatee festivities or hazard. It is a very stimulating color for use during the Christmas festival.

❻

In this example the same shapes give off different impression according to their colors. The color green here exudes the feeling of harmony or safety. Accordingly it will create a display of calm and a peaceful atmosphere. Additionally there are colors that can express advancement, retrocession, expansion and deflation. This can be seen very clearly if compared to the previous display.

❻

身のまわりにあるすべてのものは，かたちをもっています。そのかたちの中には，よく見てみると，大変に楽しいものがあることに気がつきます。この楽しいかたちもディスプレイの優れた材料です。周囲を見まわして下さい。いろいろなかたちがあるでしょう。見なれたかたち，伝統のかたち，流行のかたち，先端的なかたち，自然のかたち，不思議なかたち，意味を表わすかたち，様式のかたち，さらに，ものが動いてできる軌跡まで，ディスプレイの材料にはこと欠かないでしょう。

❶❷

　文字は，目にすることの多いかたち，見なれていること，そして意味を意識するために，かたちに気がつかない場合が多いようです。ところが意味を離れて見てみると，こんなに面白いものはありません。このディスプレイのように文字の起源を探ったり，或いは，文字を解体して使ってみると，意外な効果が生まれます。

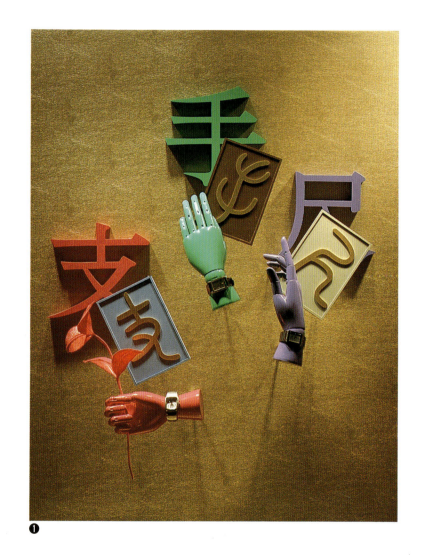

❶

SHAPES

All objects around us have their own shapes. Close inspection can reveal some very interesting shapes. Such interesting shapes become the materials for displays. Take a look around; there are many shapes just sitting there for the asking. Familier shapes, traditional shapes, fashionable shapes, pointed shapes, natural shapes, strange shapes, expressive shapes, formal shapes, even the after-prints of shapes are all objects that cannot be overlooked when constructing a display.

❶❷

Letters are the shapes which most commonly see. However, since we are familier with them and are conscious of their meanings we often forget that they are in fact shapes. If one looks at them without thinking of their meaning, it will be discovered that there is no more interesting shape available. As shown in this picture, a word broken into pieces brings out a very unexpected effect.

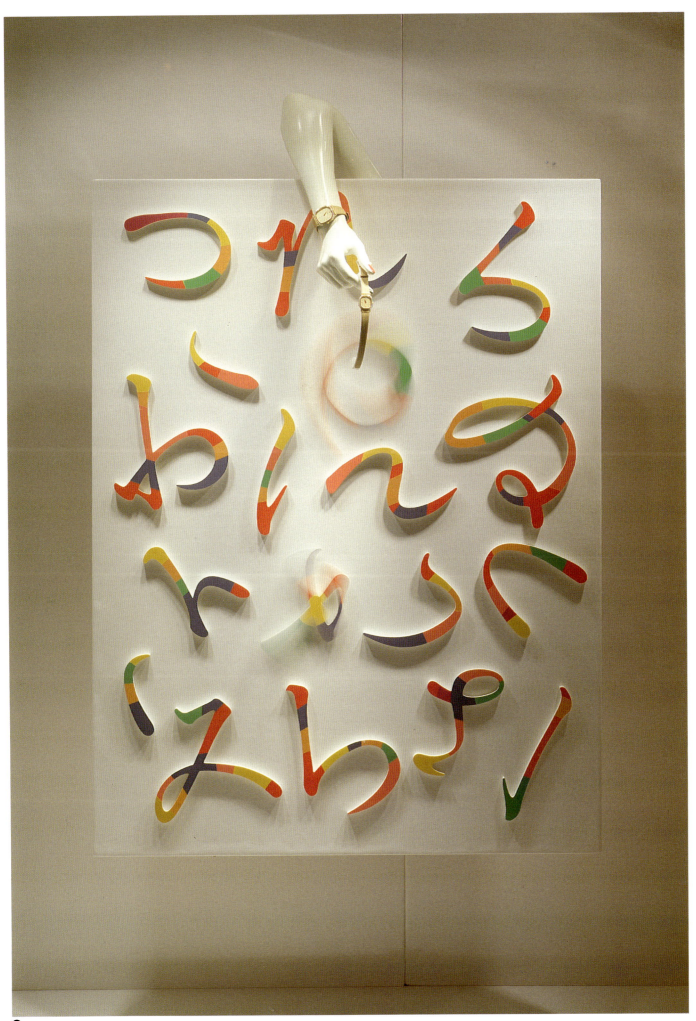

❸❹

　見なれたかたちのものも，扱い方によって
は面白いものになります。この二つのディス
プレイはその例，ただし，この場合，扱い方
に意外性が必要です。面白いものになるかな
らないかは，すべて意外性次第です。

❸❹

Even familier shapes can be made interesting according to how they are treated. These two displays offer a good example of this. It is necessary to treat them with unexpectedness in this case. The results of the shapes all depend of the character of the unexpected.

❸

TACTICS
SHISEIDO

TACTICS

After Shave Cologne

❹

59

❺❻

かたちにも流行があります。その流行の規模の大きなものが時代様式なのかもしれません。このディスプレイに使われている三角形も，このかたちの流行に合わせて使われたもの，共感を呼ぶには，効果的な材料でしょう。

❼

伝統的なかたちにもいろいろなものがあります。この青海波もその一つ，波のかたちを単純化したもののようにみられますが，その根拠は無いようです。このような伝統的なかたちは，あらたまった雰囲気をつくるには恰好の材料です。

❺

❺❻

Even shapes come under the scrutiny of popular fashion. The huge scale of fashion might be the style of all ages. The triangle used in this display has been adapted to a fashionable theme. They are effective materials for the aim of recieving the consent of the populace.

❼

Traditional shapes come in all sizes, too. This blue wave is one of them. It looks as if the actual shape of the waves have been over-simplified for no reason whatsoever. Such traditional shapes are perfect for creating a formal atmosphere.

❻

❼

⑧⑨⑩⑪

かたちの中には，固有の意味をあらわすものがあります。その代表的なものはハートのかたち，どこの国でも「愛」を表わしているようです。この意味は広がって，反戦，反暴力の意味にも使われています。

⑧⑨⑩⑪

There are also shapes that are able to express their own meanings. The most typical of these is the heart-shape which seems to be popular in all countries. Its meaning spreads over a wide area and is sometimes used to mean antiwar or anti-violence.

⑧

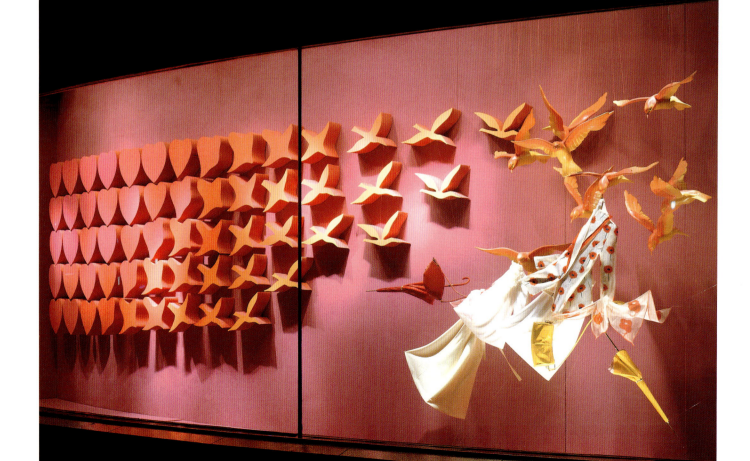

⑨

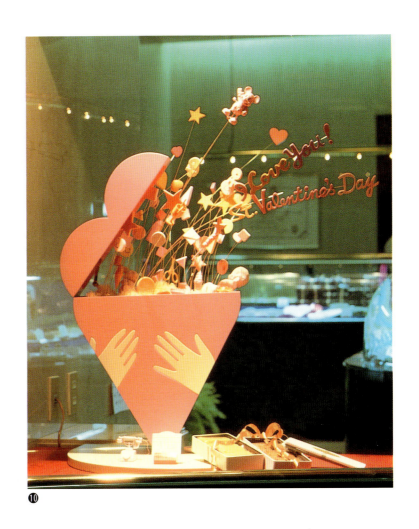

❿

⓫

MOVEMENT

人の目を捉える上で，動きほど優れた材料はありません。人の目は動きを追います。そして，少しの動きも見逃しません。

また，動きは楽しさをつくり出します。動く見世物のいろいろを思い起してみればわかるでしょう。道端の小石でも動かせば楽しくなるのです。

この動きをディスプレイにもちこむには二つの方法があります。一つは実際に動くものをもちこむこと。もう一つは動きを感じさせるものをもちこむことです。

❶❷

マリオネットは，動く見世物の代表的なもの，そのユーモラスな動きは，楽しさと共に郷愁に誘う懐かしさも持っています。長い歴史のある見世物だからでしょう。

There is no better medium for catching peoples' eyes than movement. Eyes are automatically drawn to it and never miss even the slightest movement.

Movement can create the feeling of enjoyment. A show can be easily remembered because its movement has left a permanent impression. Even a stone laying on the side of the road will turn into something interesting if it moves.

There are two methods of introducing this act of movement into displays. One is to include an object that actually does move, and the other is to use something that suggests the feeling of movement.

❶❷

The marionette is the most typical of moving shows as its humorous movement tends to bring out a yearning for our hometown with its gaiety. This could be because they are historical in character.

❶

❸

時を刻む動きも楽しいもの，このディスプレイでは，砂時計の動きによって針が動く仕掛になっています。この他にも水時計，日時計の影，振子，鳩時計の鳩と動く要素はいろいろとあります。刻々と動いていく様子は楽しいショーであることは確かでしょう。

❹

人が手を振る動きは，人目をひくものです。とくに，このディスプレイのように，動くはずの無いマネキンが手を振る姿には，思わず足を止めるでしょう。

❸

The movement of time as it ticks away is also interesting in its own right. In this display the hand moves in accordance to the egg-timer. There are many elements apart from this; stop-watches, the shadow of a sundial, a pendulum, a bird in a cuckoo clock, etc., etc. Is it not true that movement is surely interesting to watch?

❹

The movement of waving arms also attracts peoples attention. Especially in a display like this. Nobody can resist stopping if a manekin which they do not expect to move begins to wave its hands.

❸

❹

❺

動きを感じさせるものの代表は車。実際には動かなくても，今にも動き出しそうな雰囲気を感じます。その雰囲気をさらに盛り上げているのがうしろに流れているライン。スピード感を表わすパターンです。

❺

One of the most typical objects that summon up the feeling of movement are cars. Even if they are stationary they have the ability to get across a feeling of pent-up energy waiting to burst into movement. This feeling can be emphasized by the use of flowing lines in the backgound which indicate an expression of speed.

❺

❻❼

動きが，とくに印象的に見えるのは，もの
が空中を動くとき，とくに，このディスプレ
イの魔女やエンゼル達のように動きが劇的な
ものになれば，印象は更に強いものになるで
しょう。

❻❼

*Movement looks especially impressive in the
air. Like the witch and angels shown in this
play, if their movements become theatrical it
gives people a much stronger impression.*

❻

❼

❶

　緊張感をつくり出すこともディスプレイには必要です。空間をひきしめ，生き生きとしたものにする働きがあるからです。人の目を捉えるためには欠かせないものといっていいでしょう。

　この緊張感は，強く張ったもの，鋭いもの，動くもの，あぶないもの，怖いもの，光るもの，堅いものなどによってつくり出されるもののようです。この刺激的な材料をもちこんで，目が離せないといった状況をつくり出したいものです。

❷❸

　緊張感をつくり出す上で，最も活躍するものはガラス。この材料がもっている質感によるのでしょう。このガラスを割れば，さらに緊張感は高まります。そして，一種のスリラーのような雰囲気を生み出します。

❶

A FEELING OF TENSION

❶

　The creation of tension is necessary in displays. Tension has the function of tightening the given space of the display and making it seem more lively. This cannot be overlooked if the display is intended to catch the eye.

　This feeling of tension can be created by the inclussion of something sharp, moving, dangerous, scary, shiny, and so on. Stimulating materials must be used in order to ensure that peoples' eyes remain fixed on the product.

❷❸

　In terms of creating this feeling of tension, the material that creates the best feeling of action is glass. This is owing to the quality of its character. Broken glass further stimulates the feeling of tension. It can summon up the idea of a thriller movie.

❷

❸

❹

冒険物語は，スリルとサスペンスが売りもの。このスリルとサスペンスも緊張感を生み出します。このディスプレイも冒険物語，槍の穂先の鈍い光と鋭さ，盾になっている傾いた板が緊張感を高めています。

❹

Adventure stories contain a wealth of thrills and suspense. These qualities of course create a feeling of tension. This display is adventurous in its design. The dull shine and obvious sharpness of the spear and the tilting shield which is receiving its thrust have the ability to stimulate tension in people.

❹

❺

跳びはねる魚。空間を横切る稲妻のような鋭いライン。緊張感をつくり出す仕掛が揃っています。このはりつめたような場面の緊張の度を，さらに強めているのは床のガラスの冷い光です。

❻❼

綱渡りに玉のりに皿まわし。これらの曲芸は，すべてあぶなさが売りもの。このあぶなさも緊張感を生み出します。この，今にも崩れ落ちそうな椅子の曲芸も，あぶなさが見せ場になっています。

❺

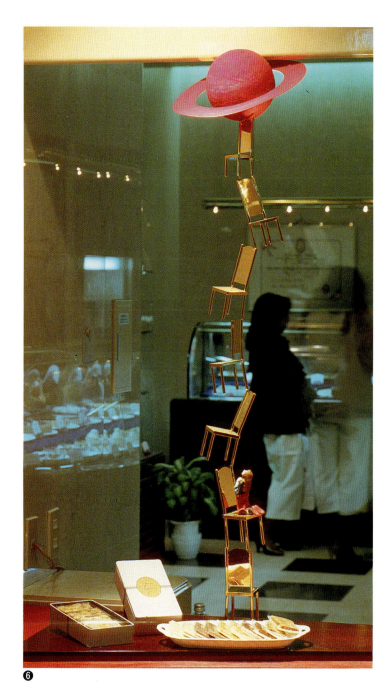

❻

A leaping fish. A sharp line that resembles a spearhead crosses the space. These are enough materials here to create the feeling of tension. And this tension is further compounded by the effect of the cold lighting.

❻❼
Tight-rope walking, balancing acts and dish-spinning; also create a feeling of tension. The dangrous acrobatic act here is the highlight of the show and tension is created while awaiting the collapse of the chains.

❼

❶❷❸❹❺

「盛りだくさん」という言葉は，楽しさの代名詞みたいなものです。たくさんあることが豊かさに通じるからでしょうか。

　この時あつめるものは，ここで使われているような野菜や果物，お菓子や酒ビンのように，普段見慣れたものがいいでしょう。たくさん集められることによって意外性が生まれるからです。この意外性をさらに強めるためにはあつめられたものを材料にして造形してみるといいでしょう。この動物や文字や模様のように。この造形物から受けるイメージと普段受けるイメージとの間のズレが意外性を強めるのです。

　揃っていることも楽しさに通じます。ラインダンスや祭の行進を思い起してみればわかるでしょう。色で揃えてみる，かたちで揃えてみる，サイズで揃えてみる，いろいろな揃え方があります。

❶❷❸❹❺

The word plenty has become a synonym for the word enjoyment. This is because it can be construed as wealth. The things that need to be gathered here are vegetables, fruit, sweets and drink bottles. The unexpected can be created by the collection of many object together. It is a good idea to make different shapes with the objects collected in order to emphasize the unexpected as in this animal, letter and pattern. A discrepancy found between an image received by this creative object and the actual object is enough to emphasize the unexpected.

An action of togetherness also lends a feeling of enjoyment. This can be clearly understood by the recollection of line-dancing or marching in a festival. There are many ways to create this togetherness; matching colors, careful contemplation of the shapes and creating sets in accordance to size.

❶

②

❸

❹

ファンタジー

　ファンタジーとは，現実にはありえない空想上のものを，あたかも現実のものであるかのように表現することです。それは，普段の生活では目にすることのできない世界を，目のあたりにすることといっていいでしょう。それだけに印象は強く，見る人を空想の世界に遊ばせます。日常から離れ，夢の世界に導くことがディスプレイの大きな働き。とすると，このファンタジーは，ディスプレイには無くてはならないものといっていいでしょう。

❶

　意外な材料を使ってみることは，ファンタジーをつくるための一つの方法。この客船の材料は炭。この材料の意外性が，このディスプレイを刺激に富んだファンタジーに仕上げているのです。

❷

　ディスプレイでは，本物に似せてつくった花よりも，この世では見られないような花を使った方が効果が高いようです。但し，その場合，できるだけ手をかけてもっともらしく作ることがコツ。そのもっともらしさが意外性を強めるからです。

FANTASY

　Fantasy is the art of making things which do not exist in real life seems as if they really do. This can offer people a glimpse into a life that they have never seen and therefore gives them a pleasant feeling of enjoyment. One of the main aims of displays is to lead people away from everyday life and into a land of dreams. This means that the existence of fantasy cannot be missed in the display area.

❶

　One of the methods of creating a feeling of fantasy in the display is to use unexpected materials. The material used to make this passenger boat is charcoal. The use of this strange material changed the display into a world of existing fantasy.

❷

　When creating flowers, it would be better to make a flower that does not exist in real life than to make one that does. If this is undertaken time and care must be expended to ensure that it does in fact look plausible. Its very viability will emphasize the character of the unexpected.

❶

❷

❸

身のまわりの身なれたものも，ちょっと手を加えればファンタジーの世界のものになります。このディスプレイがその一つの例。見なれたものだけに，かえって意外性が強く感じられます。

❹

星はファンタジーではよくつかわれる材料。夜空に輝いている星が，空想の世界に導いてくれるからでしょう。とくにハレー彗星は多くの伝説をもっているだけに想像力を刺激します。

❸

By working with the familiar objects that appear in everyday life, one can easily turn them into something that seems to belong to the world of fantasy. This display is a good example of this. The character of the unexpected is produced here all the more powerfully owing to the familiarity of the original object.

❹

Stars are often used to sum up the world of fantasy. This must be attributed to the fantastic lure of the stars shining in the night sky. Such heavenly bodies such as Halley's Comet have many legends flowing in their wake that peoples' imagination is automatically stimulated.

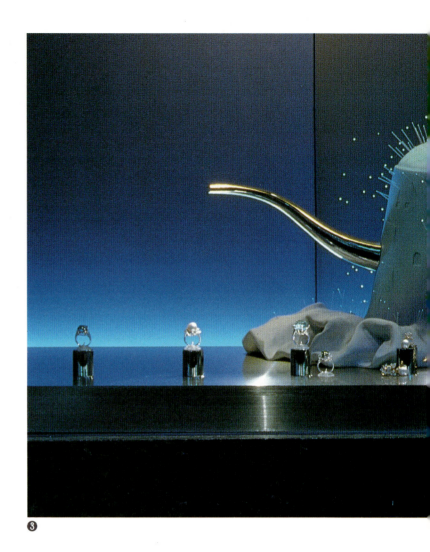

❸

❹

❺

　得体のしれない材料，得体のしれない形も
ファンタジーの世界のものでしょう。このよ
うに捉えどころのないものをつくり出すため
には遊びごころが必要です。思いきり想像の
世界で遊んでみることが，優れたファンタジ
ーづくりに結びつきます。

❻

　音楽に結びついたものも，ファンタジーで
よく使われます。音楽が想像力をかき立てる
からでしょう。そして楽器のかたちは，音を
鳴らす機能からきたものですが，何か不思議
な世界の道具のように見えることがあります。

❺

❺

*Mysterious shapes and materials belong to the
world of fantasy. In order to create something
along the lines of the outrageous one must have
the playful imagination of a child. The best
creations of fantasy will be made by those who
revel in this strange world.*

❻

*Things related to music can also be used in the
creation of fantasy. This is owing to the well-
known fact that music has a stimulating effect
on the imagination. As the shape of all musical
instruments are created in accordance to the
musical function that they must meet, they can
easily resemble strange tools from a different
world.*

❻

スポーツほど人を興奮させるものはありません。その興奮ぶりは，あらゆる場でみることができます。それは，スポーツが狩猟行動という人間の本能的なもののかたちを変えたものだからでしょう。走る，跳ぶ，的を狙う，投げる，馬に乗る，すべて狩猟のかたちです。そして，これらの行動がもたらす解放感は，スポーツだけがもっているものといっていいでしょう。

❶❷❸❹❺
スポーツの表現の一つは，このディスプレイのように，スポーツ・シーンをストレートにもちこむこと。この情景がもっている躍動美と解放感は，見る人をひきこまずにはおかないでしょう。

There is nothing like sports to get people excited. The pent-up feeling of excitement can be seen and felt in all sports. This must be owing to the fact that sports satisfy the instinctive bodily rememberance of humans as hunters. Running, jumping, aiming at the enemy, throwing, riding; these are all forms of hunting. The liberating feelings that can be gained from these actions can only be found in sports.

❶❷❸❹❺
One of the expressions of sports in to introduce a scene as in this display. The natural beauty of movement and the feeling of liberation which this scene summons up cannot help but draw the attention of people.

❶

❷

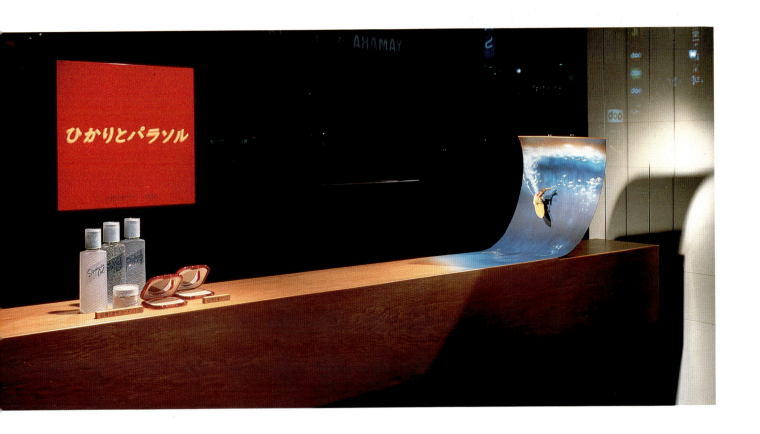

ひかりとパラソル

❸

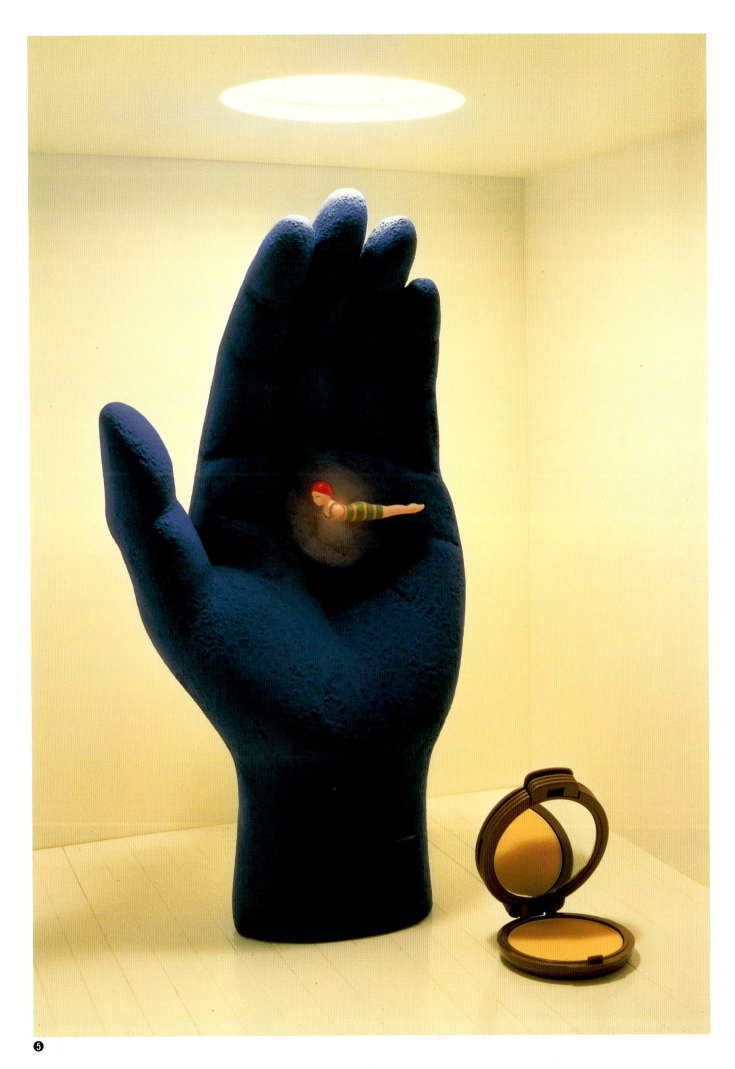

❻

旗は敵と味方を示すサインであり，士気を盛りあげる道具です。そこでスポーツに結びつきます。さらに，その旗に描かれている模様と色彩は，ディスプレイの材料としては大変に優れたものでしょう。

❼

勝利の表現もディスプレイの材料になります。その表現を代表するものは胴上げでしょう。両手をあげる，ジャンプする。勝った者同志が触れ合う，といった勝利の表現がすべてもりこまれているからです。この喜びのシーンは，見る人にも喜びを与えます

❻

Flags are symbols of indicating enemies and allies and are tools for the benefit of stimulating the fighting spirit. And so they lend a feeling of sports to any scene. The patterns and colouring of the flags are excellent materials for displays.

❼

The expression of victory is also an excellent idea for displays. The typical expression of this is the tossing in the air of a collegue or piece of equipment. It can also be got across by the actions of throwing the hands up, jumping and coming into contact with ones fellow victor. This happy scene would give the spectators happiness as well.

❻

季節の風物も関心をあつめます。なにしろ四季の移り変わりの中で生活し，そこに喜びを見出してきたのですから当然のことです。

また，季節の風物は，そのさなかにあって目にするものだけに，実感があり，共感もあります。印象が強くなるのも当然でしょう。

❶❷

春の風物の代表は花。一口に花といってもその種類は無数にあります。また，その表現も，つぼみ，咲き乱れる花，散る花，想像の花といろいろ。さらに，生の花，布の花，金属の花とあり，こんなに多彩な表現ができるものも珍しいといっていいでしょう。

Seasonal features have the ability to draw the attention of people. I suppose this is quite natural as we have always lived in harmony with the seasons and found happiness within them.

Seasonalism has special sympathetic atmospheres as they are only visited once a year. Owing to this it is quite natural for us to have strong impressions towards them.

❶❷

The typical feature of spring is flowers. The single word "flower" cannot on its own sum up the extent of its subject. And the expressions vary in accordance to the depth of the season; there are buds, flowers in full bloom, falling flowers and imaginative flowers, etc. Furthermore, there are live flowers and flowers made of material and metals. It is difficult to find something that has as many expressions as these flowers.

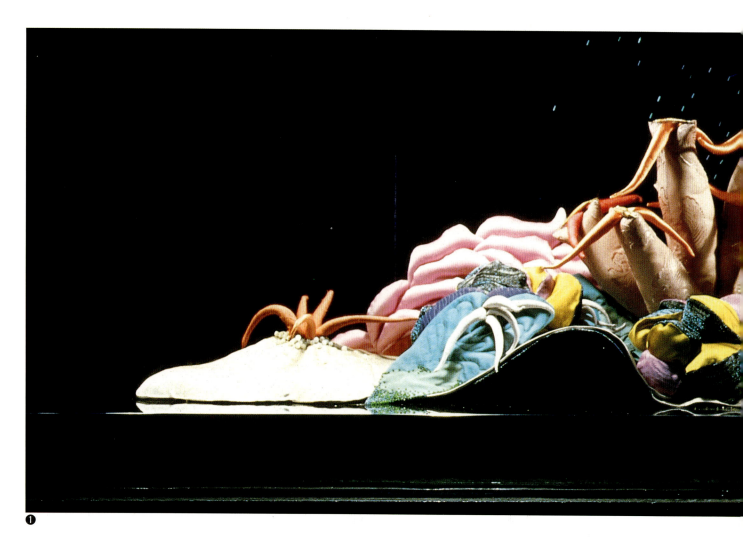

❶

❷

❸❹❺

夏は海，と相場が決まっていますが，青い
空も夏の風物でしょう。さらに南国の情景や
南国の花も考えられます。これらの風物は，
鮮やかさと爽やかさが無くてはならないでし
ょう。

❸❹❺

The ocean is considered to be a feature of the summer. Blue-skies can also be categorized as such. And, there are also views and the flowers of tropical countries. However, the feature that typifies summer the most must be brightness and freshness.

❸

❹

❺

❻

秋は実りの季節，そこで収穫のものが幅を
きかせます。この収穫のものは，できるだけ
たっぷりと使いたいもの，豊かさが，実りの
ものを際立てて見せるからです。

❼

冬の風物の代表は雪と氷。この冷たい材料
も，人の手が加われば，あたたかさを感じる
ものになります。雪だるまが，そのいい例で
す。この氷の彫刻を模したディスプレイも，
その一つの例でしょう。

❻

Autumn is the time of year for harvesting. At
this time of year harvested crops can be used.
This method should be used as much as possible
as plentifulness is a sign of harvest-time.

❼

Snow and ice are the typical features of
winter. This cold material can easily be turned
into something warm by the simple skill of
human beings. Snowmen are a good example
of this. This display which is an immitation of
an ice-sculpture is also one of the examples.

❻

❼

99

季節の行事を代表するものは祭り。これほど気分を高めるものはありません。祭りには人をまきこむ神秘的な魅力があるようです。もともと祭りとは，人をあつめ，集団の結束を図り，労働を鼓舞するという大切な働きがあるのです。それだけに，大きな魅力がなければならなかったのでしょう。

❶❷❸❹❺❻

この祭りを代表するものの一つはクリスマス。この祭りの日を表わす材料には，おなじみのものがいろいろとあります。まずはツリー，このクリスマス飾りの歴史は古く，生命の木信仰まで遡ることができるようです。その他にも，リース，キャンドル，サンタクロース，聖歌隊，と楽しさのあるものばかりです。

SEASONAL EVENTS

The most typical seasonal events are festivals and nothing can stimulate feelings better than these. Festivals possess some kind of mystical charm which drags peoples into its depths. The original festivals were important events which stimulated group activities and had the power to unite people in labor. This is one of the reasons that they have great charm.

❶❷❸❹❺❻

The most popular event of all is Christmas. As is well-known, there are many materials that are able to express this festival. The most typical is the Christmas tree. The history of this tree is so old it can be traced back to the tree of life. There are many other materials such which can provide the feeling of gaiety such as wreaths candles, Santa Claus and church-chorus', etc.

❶

❻

正月も祭りを代表するものでしょう。この
祭りを表わすものにもいろいろあります。ま
ずは門松やしめなわなどの祝い飾り，祝の膳
も華やかなものです。そして，正月遊びの道
具は楽しいものばかり。これらの材料を使っ
て，新しい年を迎える清々しさと，祭りの日
の華やかさを，いかに表現するか，これが正
月のディスプレイの課題でしょう。

*New Year is also a popular festive event.
There are many materials to express this such
as pine boughs decorating the front door, rope
decorations and special seasonal food, all of
which have the ability to produce a festive
atmosphere. The traditional games played at
New Year are also good fun. The main question
at this time of the year is how one can express
both the revitalized freshness of the coming
year and the present festivities by the use of the
above materials.*

❼

❽

❾

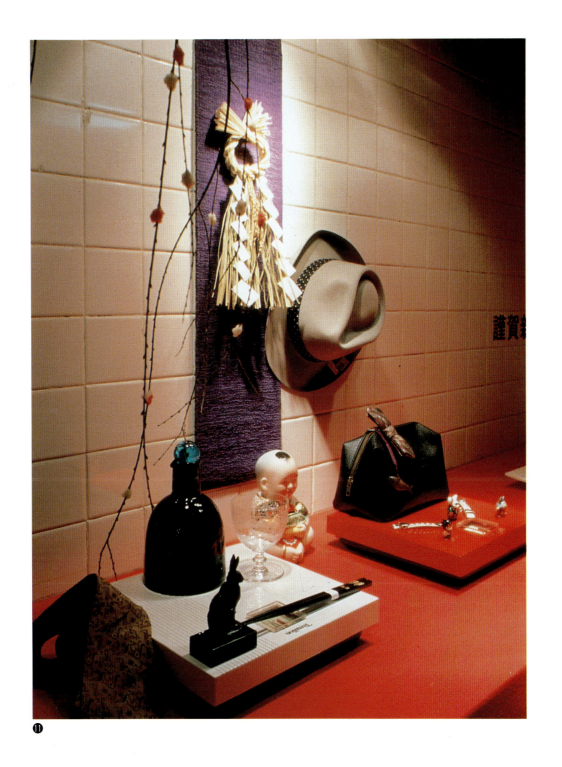

❶

❷

⓭⓮⓯⓰

祭り飾りは楽しさにあふれています。それは，この飾りが，人の気分を高める目的をもっているからでしょう。もともと祭り飾りとは，神をもてなすためのもの，そこからも楽しさが必要だったのです。ここに使われているちょうちんやまん幕，祭り人形，山車，それぞれに楽しさにあふれています。

⓭⓮⓯⓰

Festive decorations are full of fun. Just seeing them brings out a feeling of stimulation within people. The original festival decorations were intended to amuse the gods, but that is no reason why they should not do the same to people. Such items as the paper-lantern, colored curtains, festive dolls and mountain carts used in this play are all full of festive fun.

⓭

⑭

⑮

⑯

　身のまわりには，いろいろと不思議なものがあります。例えばオーロラとか蜃気楼といった自然がつくり出す不思議。或いは，トリックとかマジック，そして空想科学小説の世界。誰もが興味を示すものばかりです。いや，興味を示すだけではありません。その不思議を解き明かそうとします。人をまきこむためには恰好の材料といっていいでしょう。

❶

　マジックやトリックによく使われるものは鏡。このディスプレイに使われている鏡はハーフ・ミラーと呼ばれるもので，光を透過させる特性をもっています。その性質を利用した不思議な世界の展開です。

❷

　かくし絵とは，視覚の不思議な性質を利用した遊び。このディスプレイは，その遊びを利用したものです。この絵の中にかくされているのは30個以上の時計，ナゾときの楽しさをもった見世物です。

❶

MYSTERY

Many mysterious objects can be found in our daily life. The aurora and mirages are the actual creations of mother nature. There are tricks and magic and even science-fiction novels which are all examples of this. There is no question that these things manage to capture the imagination of people who try their hardest to discover the mysteries behind them. Such things make the perfect materials for involving people.

❶

Mirrors are often used in magic and trickery. The mirror used in this display is a half-mirror and has the characteristic of being able to absorb light. The mysterious world available to us all is there for the taking.

❷

Hidden pictures is a game that is used as a mysterious characteristic of illusion. This display is making use of this game. Over thirty clocks are hidden away amongst this picture. The solving of the puzzle is fun in itself.

❷

空想科学小説は，不思議な世界を描いた物語。この物語は4種類に分けられるそうです。一つは宇宙の物語，二つ目は過去や未来へのタイムトラベル，三つ目はロボットやサイボーグが活躍する科学冒険の物語，四つ目はスーパー人間の物語。するとここに登場しているロボットは科学冒険の物語，惑星の爆発シーンは宇宙の物語，透明人間はスーパー人間の物語の部類に入るわけです。

Science-fiction is the stories which belong in another mysterious world. These stories can be devided into four categories. The first is space, the second is time travel into the future or the past, the third is the science adventures in which robots and cyborgs are active and, finally, the fourth is about humans with super-powers. In this display the exploding planet is related to the space category and the invisible man is from the super-human department.

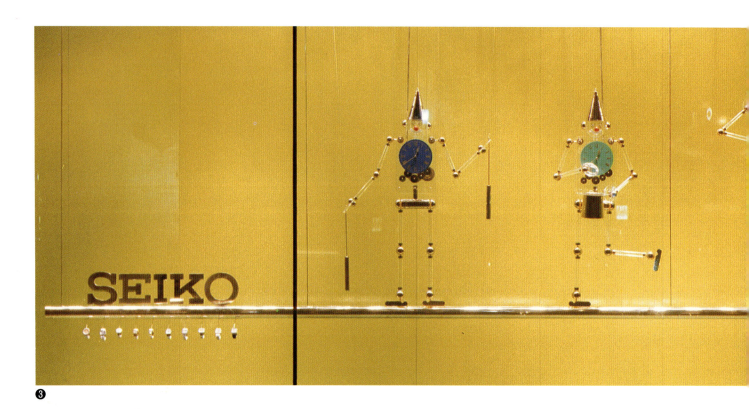

❸

❹

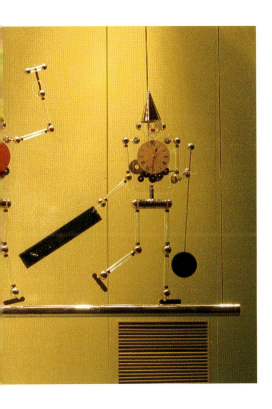

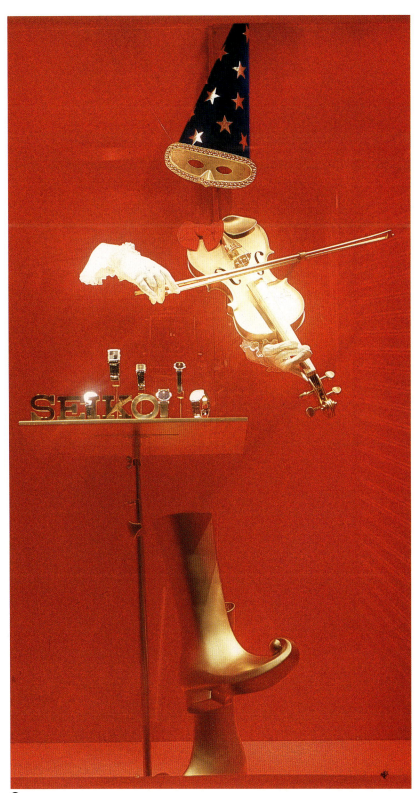

❺

異国への憧れは，誰もがもっているものでしょう。この憧れは異なるもの，不思議なものへの興味から生まれてくるものかもしれません。この興味は，人を地の涯，海の涯まで駆り立てるのです。

Everyone has a yearning to visit foreign lands. This longing stems from something different or even mysterious. Such interest has the ability to drag people to the ends of the earth.

❶

アラビアンナイトの世界はエキゾチシズムの最たるもの。この古い昔の物語は，我々を夢の世界に誘います。そして，ここでは，神輿という日本の伝統的なものをアラブ風に仕立て，意外性の面白さを出しています。

❶

The world of the Arabian Nights is one of the most exotic. This old story can lure us with ease to the world of fantasy. Here a traditional Japanese religeous chant is lent a hint of the Arabian style and the fun combination is used in a display.

❷

砂漠の情景にもエキゾチシズムを感じます。このディスプレイは，その砂漠を象徴的に表現したもの。砂の上の足跡と投げ捨てられた水筒が劇的効果をあげています。

❷

The feeling of the exotic is also found in the desert. This display expresses the desert in a symbolic way and the foot-prints and discarded water-flask adds a very dramatic effect.

❶

❷

❸❹❺

古い昔のものや，伝統的なものは，今の生活からみると，異なった世界のことのようにみえます。そこでエキゾチシズムを感じるのです。ここで使われている日傘や火の見櫓や衣裳，或いは印半纏，いずれもエキゾチシズムのあるものといっていいでしょう。

❸❹❺

Traditional objects of the past almost seems to have belonged to a different world. In this sense they have their own feel of the exotic. This fire-lookout and costume and the printed words on the workman's livery contain some of this.

❸

❹

❺

❶❷❸④⑤⑥⑦

　ノスタルジアとは，誰もが心の中に大切にしまっているもの。それが情景になって，目の当たりにされれば，感激を呼ぶことはたしかでしょう。

　このノスタルジアを誘う方法の一つは，子供の頃の思い出につながるものをもちこむこと，小石や木の棒や貝殻といった遊び道具，或いは浮輪や風鈴や西瓜の切身といった子供の頃の夏の日に結びつくもの，そして風車の遊びやクリスマスの遊び，人形遊びや手影絵遊び，すべてなつかしさのあるものばかりです。

　子供の頃読んだ物語や絵本の世界も使えます。輝く星，ムーンフェース，街の景色，いろいろと思い出の中から拾い出して下さい。

❶❷❸④⑤⑥⑦

　Nostalgia is alive and kicking within everybody. When triggered and brought to the foreground it has a deep effect on our emotions. One way to activate this trigger is to show things which were used in childhood for games; sticks and shells, etc., anything that can be related to hot summer days like tyres, water-melons or the things like pinball games at Christmas can all bring back memories. The world of picture-books that were popular for children can also be used as materials. Shining stars, moon-faces, the scenes of villages, etc., can all pluck at the strings of the memory.

❶

❷

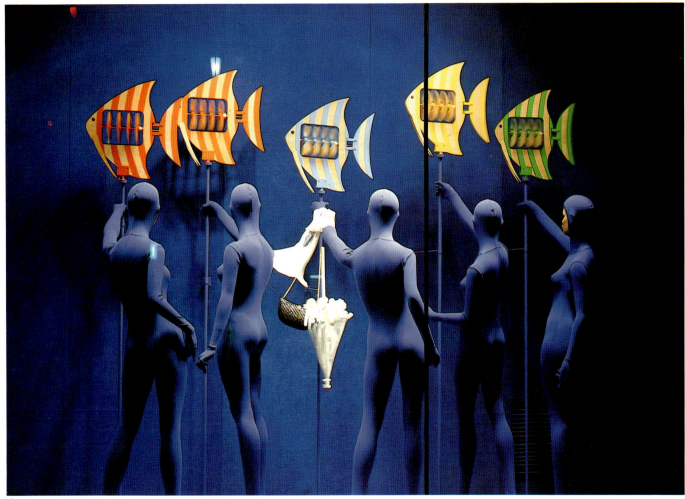

❸

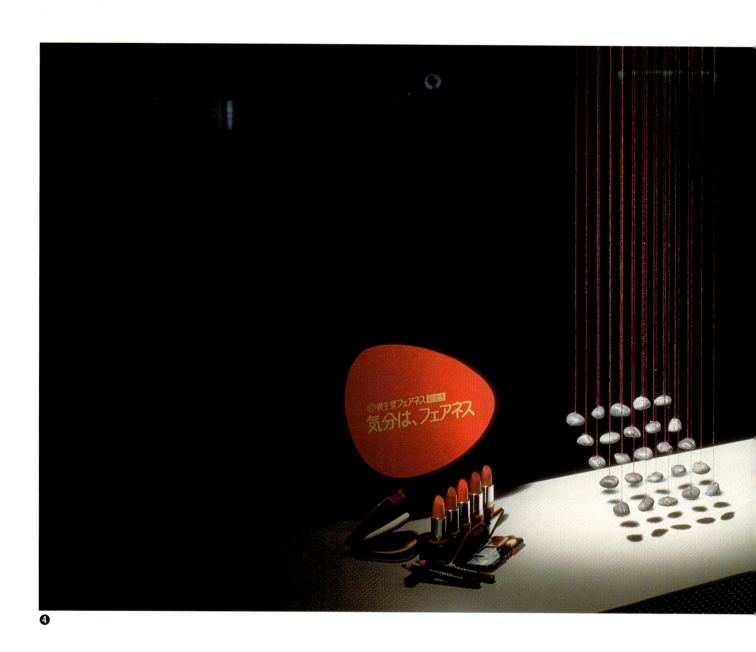

❹

❺

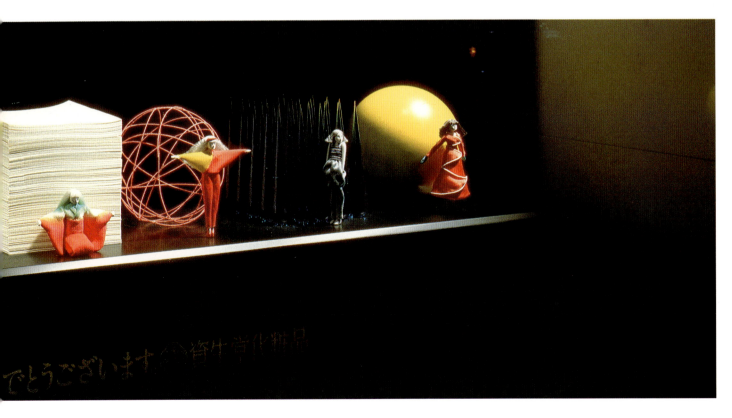

❽

❽
　ふるさとのにおいのするものを持ち込むこともノスタルジアを誘います。例えば，近頃あまり見られなくなった屋根瓦，都会育ちの人間にとってもなつかしさを感じるものでしょう。

❽
The hometown is another trigger. for example, the roofing tiles that are now alowly disapearing from the larger towns will invite a nostalgic yearning in the city-dweller.

❽
　ふるさとのにおいのするものを持ち込むこともノスタルジアを誘います。例えば，近頃あまり見られなくなった屋根瓦，都会育ちの

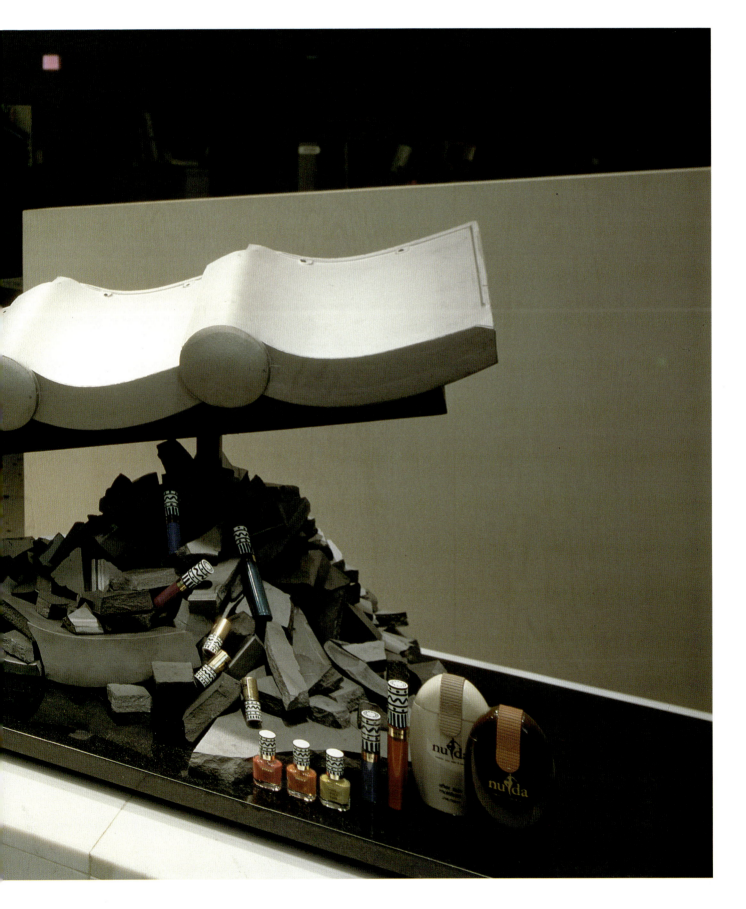

第6章　管理

管理とは，ある働きが効果をもちつづけるように取り締まることです。ディスプレイの働きは情報を伝えることであり，その目的は，行動を促すことでしたから，情報が効果的に伝わりつづけるように，そして，人が行動しやすいように周囲を取り締まることがディスプレイの管理ということになります。

情報が効果的に伝わりつづけるためには，
● ディスプレイの場とものが美しく保たれること
● 表現が常に望ましいイメージをもっていること
● 時期や期間や周期が効果的であること
この3点が必要です。そこで，質と表現とスケジュールの管理が必要になるのです。

また，効果とは，そこに投じられた経費に対して考えられるものですから，経費もまた管理の対象になるでしょう。

次に，人が行動しやすいためには，周囲の安全が必要です。そこで，安全もまた，管理の対象になるのです。

ここにあげた，質，表現，スケジュール，経費，安全，の五項目がディスプレイの管理の対象になるものです。

質を管理する

ディスプレイの場とものを，いつも美しく清潔に保つためには，汚れと埃に対する対策が必要です。

対策とは，
● 清掃のしやすさを考えること
● 汚れ難さを考えること
● 汚れを目立たせないことを考えることの3点です。

清掃のしやすさのためには，つくりものを単純なかたちにした方がいいでしょう。また，材料の選択も重要です。

汚れ難さのためにも材料が重要です。できるだけ汚れのつきにくい材料を選ぶこと，表面の粗い材料は，汚れがつきやすいので注意が必要です。プラスチックのように静電気を帯びやすい材料には防止剤の使用を忘れないように。

汚れを目立たせないためには，色と質感の選択が重要です。また，予め汚れやすいところをカバーしておくことも必要でしょう。

次に変形，変質，褪色への対策も考えなければなりません。対策とは熱と光に対するものです。ディスプレイの場は，とくに照明の熱と光の多いところ，その熱による変形と変質と，その光による褪色の起きにくい材料を選ぶべきでしょう。また，熱線を押さえた照明器具，或いは褪色防止のランプの使用も考えていいでしょう。

表現を管理する

一つの店には，数多くのディスプレイの場があります。そして，その場は休みなく活動しています。その一つ一つの表現，その一回一回の表現が，望ましいイメージに結びつかなければ，効果は期待できません。そこで表現の管理が必要になるのです。

この作業は，望ましいイメージの設定からはじまります。店の性格を基本に置き，人の行動を促進させる印象的なイメージをつくり出すのです。

次に，そのイメージに照らし合わせ，見る側に立った気持で，一つ一つ表現をチェックするのです。この時，必要なことは，イメージと表現との結びつきについての理解です。例えば，色とイメージの結びつき，かたちとイメージの結びつき，テーマとイメージの結びつきといったことの理解です。

また，このチェックの時に，キイワードやチェックリストを用意しておくと便利でしょう。

スケジュールを管理する

情報を伝えるためにはタイミングが重要です。そして，ディスプレイは，休みの無い活動といっていいでしょう。それは，店が存在している限り続きます。そこで，スケジュールの管理が必要になるのです。

スケジュールとは，時期と期間と周期の計画のことでしょう。このスケジュールを管理するとは，この時期と期間と周期によって情報伝達の効果を高め，しかも，その効果が持続するように計画し，実行することです。

商いの場のディスプレイ・スケジュールは，店の商品の計画，販売の計画，催事の計画に添って計画しますが，そこに，さらに，行事，季節の変化，ニュースなどの材料を加えて決定します。

そのとき，多彩な印象ということも考えなければなりません。この印象は，店に対する期待感を高め，生き生きとしたイメージをつくり出すからです。

スケジュールには経費からくる制約もあります。ディスプレイ一回一回の働きを考え，合理的な経費の配分も考えなければなりません。

経費を管理する

ディスプレイの効果は，他の活動と同じように，投下された経費の割合としても考える必要があります。これが経費効率です。この効率を高めるためには，経費を小さくすることを考えなければなりません。そこで，製作物，労働量，運営の三つの面からのアプローチが必要になります。

製作物の経費を小さくするためには，
● 材料の経済性
● 加工と作業の合理性
● 既製品の利用
の3点を考える必要があるでしょう。

製作物を少なくすることも考えなければなりません。無駄なものは無いか，無駄な部品はないか，効果の点を考えながらチェックしていくのです。

労働量を小さくするためには，
● 工場での製作部分を多くする
● 運搬の手間を省く
● 作業を単純化する
● 作業を標準化する
の4点を考えるべきでしょう。ディスプレイは人手を要する作業です。とくに現場での作業に人手がかかります。この人手を省くことが労働量を小さくするための課題です。

合理的な運営のためには，
● 効果的なスケジュール
● 製作物の再利用
● 変化の機能の導入
の3点を考える必要があります。

変化の機能とは，製作物や装置に，可動，交換，伸縮自在，ユニットといった機能を取り入れることです。この機能によって，変化のための経費が小さなものになるでしょう。

安全を管理する

ディスプレイの場には，数多くの危険をはらんだものがあります。いろいろな照明設備，動かすための機械，緊張感を生み出すための仕掛けなどです。この場を安全に保つためにはこれらのものの取り締まりが必要です。どんな優れたディスプレイでも，安全の約束が無ければ，効果は期待できないからです。

照明設備の取り締まりとは，配線と熱に対する配慮です。ディスプレイの場は，強い光を要求します。また，いろいろな演出照明もあります。そこから多くの配線設備が必要になります。それらを安全に保つこと，また，発生する熱を処理することが管理作業です。火災は最も恐ろしい事態ですから。

動かすための機械は，時には凶器になります。そこで，これをカバーする必要がでてきます。とくに子供は，動くものを手で触れたがります。それが思わぬ事故に結びつくことがありますから，注意を怠ってはなりません。

緊張感をつくり出すための仕掛けも凶器になることがあります。とくに，ガラスの使用には十分な注意が必要です。割れないように注意すること，そして，万一割れた時に，危険を及ぼさないような配慮をしなければなりません。

この他にも危険なものは無いか，準備の段階で，必ずチェックすることを忘れてはならないでしょう。

第7章 評価

すべての活動は，最終的に評価されなければなりません。ディスプレイも例外ではないでしょう。

評価とは，目的に対する達成の度合いを測ることです。ディスプレイの目的は，情報を伝えることによって行動を促すことでしたから，促進された行動の量を測ることが，評価ということになります。

商いの場の行動とは，購買行動です。そして，その行動の量は，売上高として表われるものでしょう。その売上高を，面積に対してと，従業員一人当りに対しての二つの量にし，その数値によって評価を行うのが一般的です。そして，その量のうち，ディスプレイによって促進されたのはどの程度なのか，その量を推測するのです。その推測は販売員の判断によるしか行法はないでしょう。時には，アンケートによって調査することもあります。

ディスプレイの場の前での客の態度も評価の対象になります。その場を，どの程度熱心に見たか，どの程度の時間立ち止まったのかを測るのです。そこから関心の度合いを測ることができます。しかし，この方法は観察によるしか判断ができません。また測る物差しもありません。評価の方法としては，あいまいなものといっていいでしょう。

次に，それぞれの場で，目的との照らし合わせを行わなければなりません。ショーウインドウの目的は，
- 情報を伝えること
- 誘引するすこと
- 選別すること
- 販売すること
- もてなすこと
- 話題づくり
- 街の景観づくり

の7点でした。

ショースペースの目的は，
- 商品のありかを知らせること
- 売場の性格を知らせること
- 商品を説明すること
- 催しものを知らせること
- 売場に鮮度を出すこと
- にぎわい感を出すこと
- もてなすこと
- 誘導すること

の8点です。

この一つ一つの目的に対する働き具合を，確かめるのです。

そして，最後に，経営結果との照らし合わせを行わなければなりません。また，目的とするイメージとの照らし合わせも必要です。ディスプレイは，これらの評価を挺子にして活動を続けて行くのです。

6) MANAGEMENT

This means the control of a certain piece of work in order to maintain or increase its effect. The main function of displays is to pass on information and, of course, to urge the consumer into action. The main responsibility of management within the world of displays is to control the input of information to ensure that it is being passed on to the best of the displays ability and to control the surroundings to make it easy of people to move around it.

The area and products available on a display should be kept in perfect condition to ensure that the correct level of information continues to be carried across to the consumer. Also, it is important that the xpression of the display always has a desirable image. Season and present-day times should come next on the list of priorities. Therefore, management should be concerned mostly with quality, expression and schedules.

The overall effect also has a deep-rooted relationship with the expenses that are invested within. This means that cost relations are also a problem for management.

A safe environment for the consumer to move around in is also necessary to ensure brisk business. Another problem for management are quality, expression, schedules, expenses and safety.

Management qualities

The area around the display and the objects upon it must be kept scrupulously clean and beautiful. Countermeasures against the threat of dirt and dust must therefore be considered. There are three main points which can be utilized to maintain this; 1) to construct the display to enable easy cleaning, 2) to construct the display in such a way that makes it difficult to become soiled, and 3) to use materials which do not make the dirt and dust stand out.

A simplicity of shpes is one way to ensure that the display is easy to clean. And, of course, the careful selection of materials is also important. Such a selection will prevent the display becoming soiled in the first place. It is better to avoid using materials with rough surfaces as these will retain the dust. Anti-static sprays should be used on plastics to avoid the collection of dust particals.

A careful selection of colors is also important in order to hide the dirt that will invariably collect. If the display is unavoidably in a location that is prone to the collection of dirt, then it is better to cover it over with a dust sheet when not in use. The next step is to consider the shape, quality and color of the products and materials. The boggest enemies of displays are heat and light. It is as well to remember that the quality and color of many object will change if subjected to constant heat or bright lihgting. As heat is generated by powerful lighting, maybe the use of slightly lower-powered bulbs would help.

Management expression

There are many kinds of displays in short and most are in the public eye twenty-four hours a day. Good results cannot be expected if the same expression is used time after time, especially if the expression does not create a desirable image. And so management must closely study expression.

This commences with the establishment of a desirable image. This image must be in accordance to the style of the shop and be designed to capture the attention of the type of consumer that the shop attracts.

Then, it is important to put oneself in the position of the shopper and unbiasedly decide whether the image carries the correct expression. Here a good understanding of the link between image and expression is needed. This means that it is necessary to see the connection between color and image, shape and image and the message of the display and image.

A convenient way to ensure that all points are covered is to tick off keywords on a checklist.

Management of schedules

A sense of good timing is essential in order to pass on the correct information. Displays are an all year round event. As long as the shop exists, so does the display. Because of this the management must have a clear idea of seasons and schedules.

The word "scheduled" really means a strategy which takes into consideration the season, the present times and the period. To be in control of this schedule means to have the correct information to pass on regardless of the season, the time or period in as effective a way as possible and to ensure that this effect is maintained.

The display schedule for a shop is made in accordance to the products available, bargain sale plans, main attractions, the change of the seasons and any relevant news, and then a decision is taken.

At the same time it is important to consider the variegated impressions which the display might give to the public. This impression will hopefully stimulate the viewer into a feeling of lively action.

Such schedules are restricted by the expenses that are entailed to maintain them, so a study of cost against sales is imperitive to make a serious consideration of functions and viability.

The control of expenses

The effect of displays are shown against a figure of the percentage of the expenses invested in them. This is known as efficiency control. It is obvious that expenses must be reduced in order to increase efficiency, so one must approach the matter from the angle of materials, labor and management.

To do this one must concentrate on the cost of the materials used to create the display, the cost of processing the display and the amount of labor used to make and maintain it. One must embark on a quest to discover cost-efficient ways to use the materials and to rationalize the process. One way of doing this is to use ready-made display materials.

One should also consider the reduction of the products displayed. It is important not to include in the display any materials that are being wasted from the point of view of effect.

There are three main points that can decrease the volume of labor; 1) increase production on the factory floor, 2) save on delivery time between the factory and the retailer, and 3) to standardize the work-flow. Displays are objects that cannot be without the interference of human hands. This is especially true for sports displays. The problem to be solved is how to do without the need of human hands in order to decrease the amount of total man-hours spent on the display.

So a rational management needs to consider the use of an effective schedule, the recycling of products and materials and the basic function of alteration. The basic function of alteration takes into account such objects that are moveable, exchangeable and flexible plus the actual units of the products and the equipment.

The control of safety

Around any display there is an element of risk in the sense that such dangers as powerful lighting, strange systems and machinery and certain tricks are involved, and this can easily lead to an atmosphere of tension. It is therefore the job of the management to make this area of risks as inviting as possible. Regardless of how wonderful the display is, there must be a total guarantee of safety in order to expect a good result.

The control of lighting brings into being the concern over the amount of loose wires and the effect of heat. The safety control of this potentially dangerous environment from which both wires and heat could cause injury is the sole responsibility of the management. It is well-known that fire is the most dreadful of all disasters.

Machines which move equipment can also be as lethal as the deadliest of weapons. Children are naturally drawn to anything that moves, so to avoid putting them in any danger special attention is needed. Small tricks can also become dangerous weapons. Extra special care must be paid to glassware to ensure it does not become broken. Prevention is always better than cure.

A thorough check on all apparatus must be made for all steps in the process of preparation.

7) VALUATION

All activities must finally rest on the laurals of their valuation. This applies to displays as well.

Valuation means the estimation of achievement based on the initial aim. The aim of a display is to urge an otherwise unexpected action by the passing on of information, so the valuation in terms of displays is the measure of the volume of an action furthered.

Action in the world of business means the act of purchasing. The value of this action is clearly stated in the final sales figures. This valuation is generally set upon the numerical value which is produced by deviding the sales into two categories; 1) for the area, and 2) for the individual worker. However, it is very difficult to judge exactly how much this volume is furthered by the display. There is therefore much difficulty in such a valuation.

The attitude of prospective customers before the display can also be used in an evaluation. This measurement can be set according to the amount of enthusiasm shown by the customers or the amount of time that they actually spend viewing the display.

The areas of their interest can also be used as a measuring stick. However, this method is only viable under close observation as it is impossible to use the measure of actual sales and is therefore a dubious way of exact measurement.

Next, it is very important to ensure that exact aims are carried out in each display area. The "aim" of show windows can be improved by following these seven main points: the passing on of information, luring, selection, selling, the gathering of topics, creation and creating a scene which can relate to the town. The aims of show areas can be improved by following the next eight points: clear indications to show exactly where the products are, specific information as to the characteristic of the shop, a clear explanation of the products available, details of the main attractions, the promotion of a special atmosphere unique to the shop, the production of the feeling fo bustle, the service and the ability to lead the customer.

The conditions to ensure the continuation of each of the aims must be maintained.

And finally, it must not be forgotten to regularly check the actual results with the management. A regular check on the aims of the display should also be made. Displays can only continue their activities if the above valuations are taken into account.

あとがき

この書のはじめにも書いたように，ディスプレイの範囲は大変に広い。それを商いの場に限ったとしても，対象とするものの数は限りなくある。ここでは，その中でも，とくに訓染みの深いショーウインドウとショースペースに場を絞り，その演出の手法の解説を試みたのであるが，書き終えてみて，さらに多くのことが必要ではないかと感じはじめた。この場もまた，広い分野と結びついているということであろう。

しかし，ディスプレイのデザインとは，想像のものを空間に具体化する企てといっていいだろう。すると，ディスプレイにとって最も重要なことは，いかに想像の幅を広げるかという点になりそうである。この書が，その想像を刺激する役割を果せれば幸いである。

なお，この書のために貴重な資料を提供して下さった多くの方に，ここで厚く御礼を申し上げたい。

また，無理な要求に快く応えて下さったグラフィック社の山田信彦様はじめ皆様にも御礼を申しあげたいと思う。

昭和63年 4 月　　八鳥治久

AFTERWORD

As aforementioned in the first part of this book, display is a technical term that encompasses a wide area. Even if it is applied only to the commercial aspects of design, the subjects included are numerous. How to Understand and Use Display focuses on relatively familiar themes, such as the design of show-windows and show-spaces. It also gives step-by-step explanations of display techniques. Although I tried to cover as many aspects of display design as possible, the scope of this book was such that I was unnable to include every element of this form of communications.

Display design is a means of realizing one's concepts and imagination in an empty space. In this respect, the most important element in display design is how an artist expresses and enhances his or her imagination. I will be very hapy of this book succeeds at improving their image power, and thus their own creative design techniques.

I would like to thank all of the poeple who assited me in compiling this book. Without their help, I never would have been able to complete the editing involved in such a grandiose project. I would also like to give special thanks to Mr. Nobuhiko Yamada, the editor at Graphic-sha, for being so patient with my writing and material delays during the production process.

April 1988

Haruhisa Hattori

INDEX

NO.	CLIENT	DIRECTOR	DESIGNER	PRODUCTION

人間 HUMANS

NO.	CLIENT	DIRECTOR	DESIGNER	PRODUCTION
❶,❺~❼ ❾~⓭	和光 WAKO	八鳥治久 Haruhisa Hattori	重村三雄 Mitsuo Shigemura	商工美術 Shoko Bijutsu
			金谷光高 Mitsutaka Kanaya	重村三雄 Mitsuo Shigemura
			山田祐照 Hiroaki Yamada	
			今野秀道 Hidemichi Imano	
			内藤大子 Hiroko Naito	
❷	銀座レカン Lécrn Ginza	坂本雅彦 Masahiko Sakamoto	坂本雅彦 Masahiko Sakamoto	ザ・ウッド The Wood
❸,❹	三越 MITSUKOSHI	小早川茂登子 Motoko Kohayakawa	末永積治 Sekiji Suenaga	吉忠マネキン Yoshichu Manequin
			山崎道夫 Michio Yamazaki	七彩 Nanasai
❽	資生堂 SHISEIDO	田中寛志 Hiroshi Tanaka	田中寛志 Hiroshi Tanaka	現代工房 Gendai Kobo

人の動作 MOVEMENT OF PEOPLE

NO.	CLIENT	DIRECTOR	DESIGNER	PRODUCTION
❶~❺	和光 WAKO	八鳥治久 Haruhisa Hattori	山田祐照 Hiroaki Yamada	商工美術 Shoko Bijutsu
			金谷光高 Mitsutaka Kanaya	
			内藤大子 Hiroko Naito	

人の気配 APPEARENCE OF PEOPLE

NO.	CLIENT	DIRECTOR	DESIGNER	PRODUCTION
❶~❸	和光 WAKO	八鳥治久 Haruhisa Hattori	金谷光高 Mitsutaka Kanaya	商工美術 Shoko Bijutsu
			石丸雅通 Masamichi Ishimaru	

人形 DOLLS

NO.	CLIENT	DIRECTOR	DESIGNER	PRODUCTION
❶,❸,❹	資生堂 SHISEIDO	田中寛志 Hiroshi Tanaka	田中寛志 Hiroshi Tanaka	現代工房 Gendai Kobo
			加藤久仁子 Kuniko Kato	
❷	銀座レカン Lécrn Ginza	坂本雅彦 Masahiko Sakamoto	坂本雅彦 Masahiko Sakamoto	ザ・ウッド The Wood

仮面 MASKS

NO.	CLIENT	DIRECTOR	DESIGNER	PRODUCTION
❶,❸,❹	和光 WAKO	八鳥治久 Haruhisa Hattori	山田祐照 Hiroaki Yamada	商工美術 Shoko Bijutsu
			金谷光高 Mitsutaka Kanaya	
			内藤大子 Hiroko Naito	
❷	ミキモト MIKIMOTO	青木智子 Tomoko Aoki	植田いつ子 Itsuko Ueda	現代工房 Gendai Kobo

光 LIGHTING

NO.	CLIENT	DIRECTOR	DESIGNER	PRODUCTION
❶,❷,❹ ❻~❾	和光 WAKO	八鳥治久 Haruhisa Hattori	山田祐照 Hiroaki Yamada	商工美術 Shoko Bijutsu
			金谷光高 Mitsutaka Kanaya	
			内藤大子 Hiroko Naito	
❸	ミキモト MIKIMOTO	小松 良 Ryo Komatsu	青木智子 Tomoko Aoki	ザ・ウッド The Wood
❺	資生堂 SHISEIDO	田中寛志 Hiroshi Tanaka	田中寛志 Hiroshi Tanaka	現代工房 Gendai Kobo

色 COLORS

NO.	CLIENT	DIRECTOR	DESIGNER	PRODUCTION
❶,❷,❺ ❻	和光 WAKO	八鳥治久 Haruhisa Hattori	金谷光高 Mitsutaka Kanaya	商工美術 Shoko Bijutsu
			池上 典 Nori Ikegami	
			内藤大子 Hiroko Naito	
❸,❹	資生堂 SHISEIDO	田中寛志 Hiroshi Tanaka	田中寛志 Hiroshi Tanaka	ザ・ウッド The Wood
				現代工房 Gendai Kobo

かたち SHAPES

NO.	CLIENT	DIRECTOR	DESIGNER	PRODUCTION
❶~❸,❻ ❾~⓫	和光 WAKO	八鳥治久 Haruhisa Hattori	金谷光高 Mitsutaka Kanaya	商工美術 Shoko Bijutsu
			内藤大子 Hiroko Naito	
❹	資生堂 SHISEIDO	田中寛志 Hiroshi Tanaka	田中寛志 Hiroshi Tanaka	現代工房 Gendai Kobo
❺,❽	銀座レカン Lécrn Ginza	坂本雅彦 Masahiko Sakamoto	坂本雅彦 Masahiko Sakamoto	ザ・ウッド The Wood
❼	松屋 MATSUYA	宮崎倉治 Kuraji Miyazaki	宮崎倉治 Kuraji Miyazaki	M&A M&A
			打良木 誠 Makoto Utsurogi	

動き MOVEMENT

NO.	CLIENT	DIRECTOR	DESIGNER	PRODUCTION
❶~❼	和光 WAKO	八鳥治久 Haruhisa Hattori	池上 典 Nori Ikegami	商工美術 Shoko Bijutsu
			金谷光高 Mitsutaka Kanaya	
			山田祐照 Hiroaki Yamada	
			内藤大子 Hiroko Naito	

緊張感 A FEELING OF TENTION

NO.	CLIENT	DIRECTOR	DESIGNER	PRODUCTION
❶,❸,❹ ❼	和光 WAKO	八鳥治久 Haruhisa Hattori	金谷光高 Mitsutaka Kanaya	商工美術 Shoko Bijutsu
		吉田和夫 Kazuo Yoshida	重村三雄 Mitsuo Shigemura	重村三雄 Mitsuo Shigemura
			池上 典 Nori Ikegami	
			内藤大子 Hiroko Naito	
❷,❺	ミキモト MIKIMOTO	小松 良 Ryo Komatsu	渡辺雅稔 Masatoshi Watan	現代工房 Gendai Kobo
❻	銀座レカン Lécrn Ginza	坂本雅彦 Masahiko Sakamoto	坂本雅彦 Masahiko Sakamoto	ザ・ウッド The Wood

たくさん PLENTIFULLNESS

❶〜❺	和光 WAKO	八鳥治久 Haruhisa Hattori	今野秀通 Hidemichi Imano	商工美術 Shoko Bijutsu
			脇田愛二郎 Aijiro Wakita	

ファンタジー FANTASY

❶〜❻	ミキモト MIKIMOTO	小松 良 Ryo Komatsu	青木智子 Tomoko Aoki	現代工房 Gendai Kobo
		青木智子 Tomoko Aoki	渡辺雅稔 Masatoshi Watanabe	アトリエあい Atelier Ai
			戸谷成雄 Shigeo Toya	
			小竹信節 Nobutaka Kotake	

スポーツ SPORTS

❶,❹,❺	資生堂 SHISEIDO	田中寛志 Hiroshi Tanaka	田中寛志 Hiroshi Tanaka	現代工房 Gendai Kobo
			一噌万左留 Masaru Isso	
				ザ・ウッド The Wood
❷,❸,❻ ❼	和光 WAKO	八鳥治久 Haruhisa Hattori	山田祐照 Hiroaki Yamada	商工美術 Shoko Bijutsu
			重村三雄 Mitsuo Shigemura	
			池上 典 Nori Ikegami	

季節の風物 SEASONAL FEATURES

❶,❹,❺	ミキモト MIKIMOTO	小松 良 Ryo Komatsu	青木智子 Tomoko Aoki	現代工房 Gendai Kobo
			渡辺雅稔 Masatoshi Watanabe	
			岡部多恵子 Taeko Okabe	
❷,❻	松屋 MATSUYA	宮崎倉治 Kuraji Miyazaki	宮崎倉治 Kuraji Miyazaki	M & A M&A
			打良木 誠 Makoto Utsurogi	
❸	銀座レカン Lécrn Ginza	坂本雅彦 Masahiko Sakamoto	坂本雅彦 Masahiko Sakamoto	ザ・ウッド The Wood
❼	和光 WAKO	八鳥治久 Haruhisa Hattori	山田祐照 Hiroaki Yamada	商工美術 Shoko Bijutsu
			内藤大子 Hiroko Naito	

季節の行事 SEASONAL EVENTS

❶,❷,⓭	銀座レカン Lécrn Ginza	坂本雅彦 Masahiko Sakamoto	坂本雅彦 Masahiko Sakamoto	ザ・ウッド The Wood
❸	三越 MITSUKOSHI	杉野 廣 Hiroshi Sugino	山下 太 Futoshi Yamashita	京屋 Kyoya
			入山美智子 Michiko Iriyama	
❹	ユニー UNY	木下一男 Kazuo Kinoshita	武部佐智子 Sachiko Takebe	京屋 Kyoya
			石川あけみ Akemi Ishikawa	
❺〜❿,⓬	資生堂 SHISEIDO	田中寛志 Hiroshi Tanaka	田中寛志 Hiroshi Tanaka	ザ・ウッド The Wood
			長谷川裕子 Hiroko Hasegawa	長谷川裕子 Hiroko Hasegawa
⓫,⓮〜⓰	松屋 MATSUYA	宮崎倉治 Kuraji Miyazaki	宮崎倉治 Kuraji Miyazaki	M & A M&A
			打良木 誠 Makoto Utsurogi	

不思議 MYSTERY

❶〜❺	和光 WAKO	八鳥治久 Haruhisa Hattori	金谷光高 Mitsutaka Kanaya	商工美術 Shoko Bijutsu
			今野秀通 Hidemichi Imano	
			内藤大子 Hiroko Naito	

エキゾチシズム EXOTICISM

❶,❷,❹	和光 WAKO	八鳥治久 Haruhisa Hottnri	今野秀通 Hidemichi Imano	商工美術 Shoko Bijutsu
			山田祐照 Hiroaki Yamada	
			内藤大子 Hiroko Naito	
❸	三越 MITSUKOSHI	山下陽二郎 Yojiro Yamashita	坂上裕二 Yuji Sakaue	京屋 Kyoya
			野口浩幸 Hiroyuki Noguchi	
❺	松屋 MATSUYA	宮崎倉治 Kuraji Miyazaki	宮崎倉治 Kuraji Miyazaki	M & A M&A
			打良木 誠 Makoto Utsurogi	

ノスタルジア NOSTALGIA

❶,❹,❺ ❽	資生堂 SHISEIDO	田中寛志 Hiroshi Tanaka	田中寛志 Hiroshi Tanaka	ザ・ウッド The Wood
				現代工房 Gendai Kobo
				加藤久仁子 Kuniko Kato
❷	松屋 MATSUYA	宮崎倉治 Kuraji Miyazaki	宮崎倉治 Kuraji Miyazaki	M & A M&A
			打良木 誠 Makoto Utsurogi	
❸,❻	和光 WAKO	八鳥治久 Haruhisa Hattori	今野秀道 Hidemichi Imano	商工美術 Shoko Bijutsu
			内藤大子 Hiroko Naito	
			山田祐照 Hiroaki Yamada	
❼	銀座レカン Lécrn Ginza	坂本雅彦 Masahiko Sakamoto	坂本雅彦 Masahiko Sakamoto	ザ・ウッド The Wood

〈著者略歴〉
八鳥治久（はっとり・はるひさ）

1936年———旧満州奉天市生まれ
1960年———千葉大学工学部工業意匠学科卒業
同　年———株式会社和光入社
現　在———同社取締役　宣伝・デザイン企画部長,
　　　　　千葉大学, 武蔵野美術大学非常勤講師,
　　　　　日本ビジュアル・マーチャンダイジン
　　　　　グ協会理事長, 日本ディスプレイデザ
　　　　　イン協会常任理事

HOW TO DISPLAY
デザイナーに贈るディスプレイ・ソース
1988年 5 月25日　初版第 1 刷発行
1989年 1 月25日　初版第 2 刷発行
1989年11月25日　初版第 3 刷発行
1990年12月 5 日　初版第 4 刷発行

　　著者————八鳥治久　ⓒ
　発行者————久世利郎

　　印刷————錦明印刷株式会社
　　製本————錦明印刷株式会社
　　写植————三和写真工芸株式会社

　発行所————株式会社グラフィック社
　　　　　　〒102 東京都千代田区九段北1-9-12
　　　　　　☎03(263)4318　振替・東京3-114345

ISBN4-7661-0457-9 C3070